Keeping Our Children's Hearts

Our Vital Priority

Steve & Teri Maxwell

CCI Communication Concepts, Inc.

Keeping Our Children's Hearts

Ordering information:
Managers of Their Homes
2416 South 15th Street
Leavenworth, Kansas 66048
Phone: (913) 772-0392
Web: www.Titus2.com

Published by:
Communication Concepts, Inc.
Web: www.we-communicate.com

ACKNOWLEDGMENTS
Scripture taken from the HOLY BIBLE, KING JAMES VERSION.

ISBN 0-9669107-6-1

Printed in the United States of America.

1   2

Cover picture of our little friend, Jonathan. Cover design by Christopher Maxwell and inside by Sarah Maxwell.

This book is dedicated to Jesus Christ, our Savior and Lord. Religion may bring about some degree of outward conformity, but Jesus Christ changes the heart.

Contents

	Preface	7
	Acknowledgments	9
1	The Need	11
2	The Heart of the Matter	21
3	Turning Our Hearts As Parents	39
4	Directing Children's Hearts — Goals and Appetites	51
5	The Foundation for Keeping Hearts	65
6	Building Parent-Child Relationships	77
7	Practicing Discipleship	95
8	The Concept of Sheltering	103
9	The Biblical Basis of Sheltering	115
10	Our Example and Instruction As Parents	129
11	Sheltering from the Negative Influences of Things	139
12	Sheltering from Negative Influences of People	151
13	Sheltering from Other Negative Influences	169
14	The Reality of Our Sheltering Choices	187
15	Encouraging Children Toward Purpose in Life	197
16	Encouraging Toward Other Positive Influences	207
17	What About Young-Adult Children?	217
18	From Those Who Have Lived It	225
19	Naysayers	247
20	Keeping Children's Hearts	259
	Additional Resources	269

Preface

We could not have written this book from a theory-only basis. We share here what we have implemented in our own parenting of eight children, three of whom are now adults, and also what we have observed in other families.

When our children were young, we were led to believe teen rebellion was to be expected. That has not been our experience with our children. What happened? Did we simply have compliant children? No, we know our children better than that. After our salvation, we began to grow in our Christian walk. The Lord led us to take the Bible as our daily direction book. This meant we also started making choices in our personal lives, and as parents, that were different from those of other people. We believe these decisions were in large measure, or even completely, responsible for our children not having to struggle with rebellion and immorality. Looking back, we have regretted none of those decisions.

We are so blessed to have enjoyed our children, to have strong relationships with them now, and to see them serving Jesus Christ. At the same time our hearts have broken as we have watched families lose their children to the world. Even if those children begin to walk in obedience, they will carry the scars of their own and their parents' failures.

We asked our three older children to write their thoughts and experiences growing up with parents who were learning to keep hearts. Each wrote a section of one of the chapters of this book. You will also find some of their quotes at the beginning of each chapter.

We have used many real stories in *Keeping Our Children's Hearts,* but we have changed pertinent information, when appropriate, for privacy's sake. Any resemblance to someone you may know is circumstantial.

Steve & Teri

Acknowledgments

In several places in *Keeping Our Children's Hearts,* we have quoted from J. C. Ryle. He was a godly pastor from the 1800s whose writings on the Christian walk have withstood the test of time. We have been blessed and influenced by his books. Our quotes come from *The Duties of Parents.*

When researching scriptural meanings for this book, we relied heavily on *Strong's Greek and Hebrew Dictionary, Vine's Expository Dictionary of Old and New Testament Words, Vincent's Word Studies in the New Testament,* and *Theological Wordbook of the Old Testament* edited by R. Laird Harris.

We are grateful for the forty-one couples who volunteered to read the manuscript of this book and give feedback on it. This group included several pastors, a medical doctor, a psychologist, and a juvenile probation officer.

Our family is always supportive of our writing efforts. Yet, we are careful to maintain our true priorities. For several months, we changed our schedule to allow us to write at night after the children were in bed. Nathan, Christopher, and Sarah were very willing to write about how they felt coming from a home that practices what we are saying in this book. Our book reviewers frequently commented on how meaningful the children's testimonies were to them.

◆　◆　◆　◆　◆　◆　◆

I know I have been raised far differently from many other homeschooled, Christian young men. I am grateful to my parents for the choices they made to keep my heart and the blessings I have reaped in my life. Christopher

◆　◆　◆　◆　◆　◆　◆

Chapter 1

The Need

"What do you do to keep your teenagers' hearts? Our young teens aren't rebellious, sullen, angry, or withdrawn – but we know we need to make a conscious effort to keep their hearts. We see a potential problem with both of our older children. We feel like we need to change, or we will have rebellious hearts on our hands. Most people would say we have the greatest, sweetest, most loving teens – but we know their hearts, and we know we're losing them." Parents of two teens

These parents understand the great need for keeping their children's hearts. While many parents are thrilled if their teens don't cause too many problems, this family realizes there is a deeper issue: who has their children's hearts? The world exerts a strong pull. It is crucial that parents understand what keeping a child's heart means and what it will cost them to do so. Then they must decide whether they are willing to make the investment.

"We live a pretty controlled life. My wife homeschools, and we keep our children with us constantly. The brethren in my

church have children who don't follow the Lord. One of them had all his children slip away. Another had a grandson who was homeschooled, but went away when he got into the work world." A dad of young children

Parents with younger children are evaluating these situations as well. They are watching the teens at church and observing them yielding to the temptations of the world. These parents are considering the choices they can make to prevent this while their children are still young. They are yearning for youths such as David, who had a heart after God's own heart. What can they do that might be instrumental in helping their children hunger for the Lord and want to walk in obedience to Him?

"Our sixteen-year-old daughter recently lied about where she was. It was a deliberate deception to make us think she was with a girlfriend. However, we caught her with a boy. We don't have her heart, and we have no idea how to get it back." Distraught parents

Does this story strike a sympathetic blow to your heart? Can you feel the concern of these parents? We expect from the tone of this note that it is the parents' focus and desire to raise a godly child who would love the Lord Jesus and serve Him all of her life. Is it possible, or are we as parents at the mercy of our children's whims?

A Christian Parent's Heart

A biblical mandate to parents in the New Testament is, "And, ye fathers, provoke not your children to wrath: but bring them up in the nurture and admonition of the Lord" (Ephesians 6:4). In accordance with this verse, we see Christian dads and moms trying to raise children who love the Lord their God with all their heart, and with all their soul, and with all their might (Deuteronomy 6:5). It is our personal goal for our children that they grow up to love Jesus Christ, to be obedient to Him, and to serve Him in all areas of their lives.

Having been a homeschooling family since 1985, we have had significant contact and interactions with conservative Christian families. We observe parents making great sacrifices in their personal lives in the hopes of ensuring that their children become godly adults. They are living on one income so that Mom can stay home with the children. They are attending conservative, evangelical, Christian churches. Many are homeschooling. It appears they are doing everything right. Still, it is common to hear about or know families who have lost their children to the world at some point.

On the other hand, our personal experience with our children has been to move through the teen and early adult years without them experiencing rebellion or moral failures. We have found this time in our children's lives to be a season of ongoing spiritual growth and maturity. They are our best friends, and we enjoy being with them. We love seeing them ministering and having a heart for serving. Rather than mopping up the pieces from the consequences of grievous sin, our adult children are moving on in their Christian walk without the baggage of rebellion and immorality. They are spiritually robust, growing in the Lord, and serving Him.

Keeping our children's hearts has, we believe, made the difference between our adult children and others' children who have not had these same positive outcomes. With their hearts, we were able to continually direct our children, through what otherwise could have been tumultuous years, to a love for and obedience to Jesus Christ. That is why we want to recommend these ideas to you.

In this book, it is our desire to present what we see to be a biblical way of bringing up our children in the nurture and admonition of the Lord (Ephesians 6:4). This is a path that we observe being directed and supported by Scripture, beginning in early childhood or even infancy.

We started down this avenue in raising our older three children, who at the time of this writing are 27, 24, and 22. You will hear from them in a later chapter. We are continuing in this direction, in a more knowledgeable and concerted way, with our younger children, who are now 14, 13, 11, 9, and 7. We have had no regrets that we made these difficult choices. Our children haven't regretted the "keeping hearts" decisions we made for their lives either.

From our early parenting years, before we began learning what we are writing about in this book, we have some regrets, though, and so do the older children. These regrets came from experiences before we knew, or were brave enough, to stop listening to those around us – even many in the church. We had to learn to heed Scripture for our direction and answers rather than observing what others were doing. Instead of rationalizing away this verse or that verse, we began seeing their importance in our daily lives and decision making. We chose to believe and obey Scripture rather than conforming to what others were doing. In the process, we discovered the joys of being piloted by the Lord Jesus and that His ways are not our ways (Isaiah 55:8).

We would encourage you to prayerfully consider what we have to say, evaluating it against Scripture. We frequently hear and read stories of sorrow from parents who have lost their children's hearts. Sometimes a young parent asks us questions concerning keeping the hearts of their children, but doesn't like our response. We suggest they consider what they will reap in fifteen years as a result of their choices.

It is our plan to share with you concepts that may be totally foreign to your thinking, ones that you have never considered before. If you have thought about them, you might not have been convinced that it is possible to raise children while still keeping their hearts. Perhaps you have given up. We would like to propose that you consider these other options now being set before you.

Two Main Thrusts

We believe the critical factor for most families in successfully raising children in the nurture and admonition of the Lord (Ephesians 6:4) is whether or not the parents have their children's hearts. We will investigate two main thrusts to keeping hearts.

The first one involves turning our hearts toward our children (Malachi 4:6, Luke 1:17). That is the starting point. We have so many opportunities to turn our children's hearts, throughout their childhood years, to the Lord and to us, their parents, simply by turning our hearts toward them. What will we do with this opportunity? Where is our focus?

The second thrust has to do with sheltering our children from negative influences while giving them purpose and direction in life. Will we keep our children from influences, even ones that others deem harmless – those that don't edify? Will we minister with them, drawing their hearts into loving service for Christ? Will we encourage them to learn to work and keep them busy? Will we wait until it is too late to begin?

What goals do we have for our children? How do those goals impact what happens in our homes concerning them? Every decision we make that involves the children must be evaluated in light of those goals. Will this further the achievement of the goal, or will it hinder it? Are our actions and decisions consistent with the goals? What kind of appetites might it develop in my child even if the activity itself seems innocent at the time? Is my decision based on Scripture, or is it made because I don't want to be inconvenienced or disappoint anyone? Have I prayed about it, seeking God's wisdom and direction? Am I convinced this is God's will?

Avoiding negative influences while having biblical child-raising goals brings us to another aspect of keeping our children's hearts. This has to do with directing their time and efforts in beneficial directions, giving them purpose in life. If they are to avoid influences that will pull their hearts away from the Lord, what are they to do with their time? Are they learning to spend quality time with the Lord in Bible reading and prayer? Will you give your children a solid spiritual foundation through family Bible time? Do your children know how to work? Have they learned to love to serve? Not surprisingly, when our children's lives are filled with spiritual growth, productive work, and a desire to serve, there is hardly any time left over to want to be involved in negative-influencing activities, let alone to participate in them.

The Challenge

Please understand, we are not saying categorically that any child who is exposed to negative influences will be rebellious. Neither will every child who has parents who don't "walk worthy of the Lord" (Colossians 1:10) fall into immorality. Obviously there are children who make it through their teen years focused on Christ despite the pull of the world. Yet, how many do you know in that category? Are the Christian teens you come in contact with characterized by godliness or worldliness? What have you personally noticed?

If we allow our children to be influenced by the world before the Lord has sufficiently prepared them, will they be pulled to the world or stand firm for holiness? Christians want to think their children will be strong soldiers of Christ, but the reality of our observations is that this is true of very few. What does this mean to us personally, and what impact should it have on how we raise our children?

We are challenging you to evaluate what causes some parents to lose their children's hearts while others are able to keep them. We would like to look carefully at these aspects of a child's life. Having personally seen discrepancies within conservative Christian homes, we have asked questions and delved into what influences cause children's hearts to be kept or lost. We hope that Christian parents will not think that they can keep their children's hearts while allowing negative influences in their lives. Instead, we would love to see parents who are aware of influences on their children's hearts – positive and negative – and are willing to make changes in order to keep their children's hearts even if it is costly in time and effort.

We want to back up what we say with Scripture. In addition, we will encourage readers toward the importance of God's Word in their lives on a daily basis, personally and as a family. If we want to keep our children's hearts, it is not done apart from relying on God's truth and His direction. Every decision we make has to be held up to the filter of the Bible.

We would like to show you the positive results of choices leading to keeping our children's hearts as contrasted with the frequent negative results of not making these kinds of decisions. We desire that each reader would be encouraged that there is great joy and blessing in bringing up children in the nurture and admonition of the Lord. Finally, we want to give parents a beautiful, realistic picture of raising children, in a Christian home, who will love and serve Jesus Christ with their whole hearts all the days of their lives.

Questions

1. How important do you believe keeping a child's heart is for avoiding teen rebellion and immorality?

2. Is it possible for parents to keep a child's heart?

3. When would keeping a child's heart begin?

4. What factors do you think go into keeping a child's heart?

5. What factors will hinder keeping a child's heart?

6. Do you want to keep your child's heart?

7. How much time and effort would you be willing to invest to keep your children's hearts?

8. How likely do you think it is for a child to rebel in his teens if you don't have his heart?

   a. Is it worth taking the risk of him rebelling?

♦ ♦ ♦ ♦ ♦ ♦ ♦

*I had a normal childhood. I don't have regrets
about what I could or couldn't do. My childhood is
full of happy memories. Nathan*

♦ ♦ ♦ ♦ ♦ ♦ ♦

Chapter 2

The Heart of the Matter

Why would we want to keep our children's hearts and expend great effort in doing that? What difference does it make? What exactly does it mean to have their hearts? How will we know if we have kept our children's hearts? These are vital questions to ask and to answer as we delve into keeping hearts.

My Son, Give Me Thine Heart

The primary verse we think of when the subject of keeping a child's heart is discussed is Proverbs 23:26. "My son, give me thine heart, and let thine eyes observe my ways." Solomon was the richest man in the world, yet there was still a treasure he sought from his son. Why did Solomon ask his son to give him his heart? Could it be there was some further wisdom to be gained by having his son's heart? No, of course not. What exactly was Solomon requesting by wanting his son's heart?

Solomon was addressing his son. The word "son" in Hebrew literally means "to build." It is used figuratively of one's house, thereby actually referring to one's children. What a beautiful picture this presents of a man actively involved in the building and shaping of a child.

Looking at the word "heart" in Hebrew, we see it refers to the center of a person's understanding, emotions, mind, soul, appetites, passions, and courage. In essence, Solomon wanted his son's emotional and mental being.

Solomon used the word "give" in asking for his son's heart. However, the tense of the word indicates that it was actually a command. As a parent, he knew what was best, and he was insisting that his son give him his heart.

Solomon goes on to say, "Let thine eyes observe my ways." The Hebrew word for "eyes" literally means eyes, but it can also figuratively refer to "one's mental and spiritual abilities." It is the word used in the Garden of Eden when Adam and Eve's eyes were opened to good and evil. It is also found in Proverbs 4:25: "Let thine eyes look right on, and let thine eyelids look straight before thee." Here we see that it represents one's moral faculty.

"Keep thy heart with all diligence; for out of it *are* the issues of life" (Proverbs 4:23). Solomon knew that the heart is where the battle rages and sets the course for life. He realized that if wrong youthful appetites are allowed to flourish, the child's life could be shipwrecked.

Because of Solomon's love and concern for his child's well-being, he was instructing his son to trust him with his very soul. He wanted his son to study his father's way of life and embrace what his father embraced as being good and profitable. Solomon was saying, "Son, esteem me such that you will take my way of life to be your own. Adhere to my example and live in the pattern that I am setting before you. Listen to my counsel and observe my ways."

Why Do We Want Their Hearts?

We want to have our children's hearts because we desire to direct those hearts to Jesus Christ. When we have a child's heart, we have the ability to influence that heart. Our ultimate goal as Christian parents is to bring our children up in the nurture and admonition of the Lord (Ephesians 6:4). We should point them to Jesus Christ. Having the child's heart, we have personally found the goal is attainable. If we don't have the heart, the child will likely be lured and pulled to the attractions of the world. While we may be able to prevent them from following these seductions when they are little, that begins to change as they reach their teen and adult years.

Parenting will be accomplished predominantly by authority if we don't have our children's hearts. This is fairly simple when the children are young. We can tell them what to do while controlling virtually every aspect of their lives. Parenting by authority becomes more difficult and tentative as children grow older. However, if we have their hearts, we find that we are able to influence our children on the basis of our relationship. Like Solomon, we can encourage the children to watch our ways. This is a powerful and successful way of parenting, particularly when we are talking about bringing our children to a relationship with Jesus Christ and discipling them for a lifetime of obedience to Him.

We want our children's hearts so that we can teach them to walk in holiness. The book of Proverbs is filled with verses describing what Solomon wanted to encourage his son to let into his heart and verses warning him what to be on guard for and reject. This kind of teaching is most successful when we have the child's heart. We have a brief list of both types to give you an idea of what to look for as you read Proverbs.

Here is a partial list of what to let into the heart:

4:1 "Hear, ye children, the Instruction of a father . . ."

4:2 "For I give you good doctrine, forsake ye not my law."

4:5 "Get wisdom, get understanding: forget it not; neither decline from the words of my mouth."

4:10 "Hear, O my son, and receive my sayings; and the years of thy life shall be many."

4:13 "Take fast hold of instruction; let her not go: keep her; for she is thy life."

4:20 "My son, attend to my words; incline thine ear unto my sayings."

4:25 "Let thine eyes look right on, and let thine eyelids look straight before thee."

Here is a partial list of what the heart should reject:

4:14 "Enter not into the path of the wicked, and go not in the way of evil *men*."

4:15 "Avoid it, pass not by it, turn from it, and pass away."

22:24-25 "Make no friendship with an angry man; and with a furious man thou shalt not go: Lest thou learn his ways, and get a snare to thy soul."

23:20 "Be not among winebibbers; among riotous eaters of flesh:"

23:26-27 "My son, give me thine heart, and let thine eyes observe my ways. For a whore *is* a deep ditch . . ."

The reason we want our children's hearts is so that, like Solomon, we can help them with what they should let into their hearts and what they should avoid. We will be direct ing them in the way of righteousness. Our main goal will be to draw our children to the Lord Jesus Christ. Then we want them to learn to be obedient to Him and to His Word. If we keep our children's hearts, this is much more possible than if we have lost their hearts.

Don't We Naturally Have the Heart?

A question begs to be answered: Doesn't the parent naturally already have his child's heart? It might be assumed that in a normal parent-and-child relationship, the parent has the child's heart. However, this isn't always the case and can be observed by a child's reaction to his parent and vice versa in various situations.

We can go back to the "garden" for an explanation. The relationship between Adam, Eve, and God was a beautiful one when it began. However, with the knowledge of good and evil came sin and a break in the relationship. Ever since, God has sought a relationship with man.

Now picture the infant in his parent's embrace. Surely, the parent naturally has the heart of the child at this early stage. Over time, as the child grows in his own knowledge of good and evil, he will make choices that are contrary to the wishes of the parent. Through the years, as the child gets "smarter," Dad and Mom seem "dumber." This begins a process of the child, by choice, toward separating his heart from his parents.

Also, consider from the parent's perspective that the cute, cuddly infant who is so loveable begins down a different path once the first "No!" is uttered. The parent's right to direct has been challenged, and the struggle begins. The natural heart-pull of the parent may start to be eroded by the ongoing defiance of the child. With a distancing of the parent's heart from his child, it is likely that the parent's interest and attention is pulled to things other than child rearing.

The child is aware of the distancing of his parents' hearts, and this affects his heart attachment to his parents. Finally, the result is the sad state of affairs that we observe in what is termed "normal" parent-child relationships. Rebellion abounds because the parent no longer has the child's heart. A child who doesn't go through a time of rebellion is considered the exception. However, rebellion is far from God's will for our children.

While it is obvious that children's hearts are naturally turned toward their parents, it is also evident that there is a process set in motion from infancy that causes a pulling away of those hearts. Our desire in keeping our children's hearts is to stop and reverse any moving away of our children's hearts from us, and of our hearts from our children. This will involve effort on our part to keep our children's hearts.

Positive Characteristics of a Kept Heart

We might glean some desirable aspects of an ideal parent-and-child relationship by looking at the one perfect relationship given to us as an example from Scripture. God the Father certainly had the "heart" of His Son, Jesus Christ. "Then answered Jesus and said unto them, Verily, verily, I say unto you, The Son can do nothing of himself, but what he seeth the Father do: for what things soever he doeth, these also doeth the Son likewise" (John 5:19).

If the parents have kept the child's heart, it will be greatly attached to the parents just as Christ's heart was attached to His Father. A child whose parents have his heart will be looking to the example of the parent. That child will respect his parents and will want to emulate them (John 5:19).

The child wants to spend time with the parent because they have common interests and life purpose. He desires to learn from the parent. ". . . I do nothing of myself; but as my Father hath taught me, I speak these things" (John 8:28). We would expect to see a child who has a close, intimate relationship with his parents if the parents have his heart.

Could there be times when the child does not want to do what the parents ask even though the parents have his heart?

What would you think the child might do? Here is Jesus' example. "He went away again the second time, and prayed, saying, O my Father, if this cup may not pass away from me, except I drink it, thy will be done" (Matthew 26:42).

Having our children's hearts doesn't mean they instantly receive everything we tell them. At times we wish that was the case, but it hasn't been our experience. However, we think it means that we can talk on a very deep and intimate level, and they will listen carefully to what we say. It means they value our words, and what comes from our hearts will weigh heavily on their souls. However, if a parent cannot give logical, spiritual, or biblical reasoning in guiding his child, that parent may simply be viewed as self-centered.

One of our sons was very interested, as a teen, in being an airplane pilot or an emergency medical technician (EMT). As Steve discussed those professions with our son, he asked him if he thought the Lord would have him marry at some point. The son said yes. Then Steve encouraged him to consider how difficult those two careers can be on a marriage. Pilots have demanding schedules, involving long hours and nights away from home, impacting a family. EMTs not only have hard work hours, but they are often paired as a man-and-woman team. This was not the positive career encouragement our son wanted to hear. However, since we had his heart, he was open to praying about this discussion and information. He has not chosen to pursue being a pilot or EMT.

Parents who have the heart of their child should see the child still obeying the will of the parents, even when it is not the desire of the child. In obeying we won't see a bitter spirit in the child but a willing heart, just as we see Christ's obedience in going to the cross. Although the Scripture used was relating to the perfect parent-and-child relationship, we should see signs of such willingness in a relationship where the parent has the heart of his child.

Recognizing a Child Whose Heart Is Not Kept

Scripture not only gave us the perfect picture of a parent who kept His Son's heart, but also an example of a father who lost his son's heart. David did not have Absalom's heart, and the consequences were disastrous. Why did he not have his son's heart?

In 2 Samuel 13, we see that David had not protected his daughter Tamar nor dealt judiciously with the injustice done to her by her brother Amnon. "And, ye fathers, provoke not your children to wrath: but bring them up in the nurture and admonition of the Lord" (Ephesians 6:4). Likely, Amnon wasn't punished because David still had guilt from his sin with Bathsheba and the subsequent murder of Uriah. This hindered David's conscience from administering justice to Amnon. It may also have kept David from having a heart fully turned to his children. In reaction to that, his children's hearts weren't turned toward him.

Absalom was bitter toward David because David could have prevented what Amnon did to Tamar. To make matters worse, David had done nothing after he heard about it. A child will look to his father to be the protector – one who safeguards the family from harm and who brings about family justice. Resentment will likely result if a father fails to fulfill his responsibility. Had David's heart been turned toward his children, he could have prevented what happened to Tamar, Amnon's murder, and Absalom's rebellion.

If parents don't have their child's heart, that child won't listen to his parents, won't value their words, and will be argumentative. He will challenge what his parents say and any decision they make that displeases him. While all children tend to be focused on themselves, this child will be even more self-centered. Rather than looking to his parents for direction and counsel, he will be proud and arrogant. As he grows older and gains more freedom, he may begin to act deceitful and lie when doing things he knows his parents wouldn't have let him do. He justifies his wrong actions and views his parents negatively because "they don't understand." Ultimately, he may lead his siblings in rebellion against the parents. Such a scenario brings grief and heartache.

A Drifting Heart

Why is having our children's hearts so important? Aren't they going to grow up anyway? Yes, obviously, they are going to grow up, whether we have their hearts or not. However, if we don't have our children's hearts, we miss out on the tremendous blessing of our children as they mature. We stand the very significant chance of losing them to the world.

The parent dedicated to keeping a child's heart is like the shepherd who is constantly inspecting his flock. He knows the danger that comes if disease or pestilence takes root, so he is quick to identify their onset. If he misses the warning signs, the toll to restore the flock to health will be high, if the shepherd is even able to accomplish it. If we have our child's heart, we can quickly tell when it is being drawn away. We will sense a heart change and know something is wrong.

When the parents keep the hearts of their children, it is very easy to see if the children's hearts begin to drift. Living with the children every day and having frequent interactions with them shows their responses and reactions to what their parents are saying. If we sense and observe a distancing of a child's heart from ours, we will begin doing what we can to draw his heart back to us. Generally, what we have discovered is that more one-on-one time is needed to bring the heart back. This gives us the opportunity to talk about what is happening. It also allows us to rebuild a struggling relationship and to express a great deal of love to the child.

There was a time when Steve felt that the heart of one of his children was slipping away. During their weekly discussion times, there were more issues of increasing difficulty to work through. Steve could see the child was struggling instead of being able to receive our concerns.

Steve was perplexed because he couldn't figure out what was going on. He began crying out to the Lord and seeking

Him for answers. The Lord showed Steve that there had been a lot of homeschool graduation social functions, and the child was spending far more time with other youth than ever before. Steve shared with this child that he believed the time with others was the real issue, and the child was able to receive it. We were blessed that the socials were over, and soon, the sweetness was back in the relationship. Hearts were close again.

If Steve hadn't had his child's heart, he would not have noticed the drifting of this child's heart. He would have thought that this was normal separation behavior and attitudes for children as they grow older. Likely, he would have believed the lie that you should accept this and not worry about it. Then the downward spiral would have continued, with the relationship deteriorating. Since Steve had his heart, that wasn't the case.

It is important to be watchful for drifting hearts and then to take steps to draw those hearts back. Sometimes we might use a lunch out with Dad or making dinner with Mom as the opportunity to discuss things on a deeper level and resolve the heart issue. Other times we may need to make major modifications in our lifestyle to recapture a drifting heart. We must be determined to invest the time to pray to discern the cause of the drifting heart and then make the necessary changes.

The Lord's Working

We have no hope of keeping our children's hearts aside from the Lord's working in our lives and in their lives. "For it is God which worketh in you both to will and to do of *his* good pleasure" (Philippians 2:13). When our children grow to be mature men and women of God, it is the Lord Who is doing the work in their lives. It is important as you read this book that this premise is understood. We are sharing what we did in raising our children that allowed us to keep their hearts, but it is the Lord's work and His doing. We were simply being obedient to what we saw as the Lord's directions for us as parents.

By keeping our children's hearts, we can be responsible to God's command to ". . . provoke not your children to wrath: but bring them up in the nurture and admonition of the Lord" (Ephesians 6:4). If we don't have their hearts, they will be provoked to wrath in following the parent's direction for them toward holiness when it is contrary to their personal wants and wishes. Keeping our children's hearts is an important aspect of bringing our children up in the nurture and admonition of the Lord. The Lord is the One doing the work. We strive to fulfill the responsibilities and duties He has delegated to us as parents. He does the rest.

Part of our responsibility in bringing our children up in the nurture and admonition of the Lord will be a continual focus on prayer for them. We should be praying for them to receive that which edifies and reject that which harms. Praying to keep our children's hearts can be a major thrust of our prayers for them. We commit ourselves to doing everything in our power to raise godly children, while crying out to the Lord to work in their hearts. Prayer is evidence of our dependence on God to do the work. Keeping their hearts enables the Lord to use us as His instrument in their lives.

Salvation

Our main goal for keeping our children's hearts is that we might first lead them to a saving faith in Jesus Christ and then to spiritual maturity. Also, keeping a child's heart will be difficult if that child does not become saved. When they are lost, their goals and purposes in life are at enmity with God's and yours.

All of our children were saved between the ages of five and seven. It seemed that because we had the children's hearts, they wanted to be like Daddy and Mommy. Salvation naturally came up in conversation on a regular basis. For each child, there was a time when he became vitally interested in being saved.

When a child persisted in his questions about salvation, it was clear to us that he was ready to be saved. Steve would talk to him and discuss salvation, making sure he had an understanding of what it meant and how to be saved. Then when Steve was confident of a proper understanding of salvation on a child's level, both of us would pray with the child for him to place his faith in Jesus Christ as his personal Lord and Savior.

"And Jesus called a little child unto him, and set him in the midst of them, And said, Verily I say unto you, Except ye be converted, and become as little children, ye shall not enter into the kingdom of heaven" (Matthew 18:2-3). "And they said, Believe on the Lord Jesus Christ, and thou shalt be saved . . ." (Acts 16:31). "That if thou shalt confess with thy mouth the Lord Jesus, and shalt believe in thine heart that God hath raised him from the dead, thou shalt be saved. For with the heart man believeth unto righteousness; and with the mouth confession is made unto salvation" (Romans 10:9-10). Based on these verses, we felt comfortable with our children being saved at young ages.

Their Hearts

We want to have our children's hearts because, as we saw with Solomon, when we have their hearts we can lead and direct them in the paths of righteousness through influence. Without having their hearts, we must rely on our authority to direct. This authority is often only effective as long as we are watching and while the children are young enough to accept our authority. However, the power of influence works from within rather than without, and through all ages. When we have our children's hearts, they want to do what is right even without being directed to do so.

Having our children's hearts, we experience a close, intimate relationship with them. If you don't have this, you are missing out on one of the greatest joys of life. Our children will value our words and direction in their lives even though they may not always agree. Because of the relationship, they know that our goals are for their best, and they will defer to their parent's wisdom. Keeping our children's hearts is dependent on the Lord's working in their lives. By having their hearts, we can more easily lead them to faith in Christ, "For with the heart man believeth unto righteousness . . ." (Romans 10:10). Then we can fulfill our responsibility to raise our children in the nurture and admonition of the Lord.

Questions

1. Do your children tend to argue with you?

2. Do your children prefer to spend time with you?

3. Do you think you have your children's hearts? Why? Why not?

4. What characteristics of a kept heart do your children exhibit?

5. What characteristics of a drifting heart do your children have?

6. Are you praying to keep your children's hearts?

7. What might you be missing if you do not have your children's hearts?

♦ ♦ ♦ ♦ ♦ ♦ ♦

Mom has cultivated a wonderful mother-and-daughter relationship with me. Sarah

♦ ♦ ♦ ♦ ♦ ♦ ♦

Chapter 3

Turning Our Hearts As Parents

We were eating dinner at an out-of-state homeschooling convention when a sixteen-year old young man asked if he might sit in the empty seat next to us. "You are welcome to as long as you don't mind us asking you a ton of questions," we answered. He agreed, he said, as long as we didn't mind if he ate. Chuckling, we surveyed his plate. It was what you would expect of a teen boy with an appetite, lip-lopping full without a square inch of empty room. As Randy sat down, we observed in him a young man with a confident smile who looked accustomed to working hard. Randy commenced eating while we began launching questions his direction. How old was he? How many in his family? How did he spend his time? What did he like to do? What sort of friends did he have? As soon as he answered one question, we had another for him.

Randy's Answers

Randy's replies were not only courteous, but also full of respect. The more we listened to his answers, the greater appreciation we had for his parents and what they were doing in his life. We could hear how much he enjoyed his family. He truly loved his parents and his siblings.

Randy's favorite person to be with in the entire world was his father. He also had one good friend, a young man in his twenties with a construction business. He really enjoyed working with his friend and learning the trade. Randy was always busy. Most boys his age would be on every sports team they could find. Not Randy. His time was filled with working with his friend, helping around home, and being with his family.

We told Randy we really wanted to meet his father. He pointed with his chin and said he was sitting right behind us. Unfortunately, as soon as we were finished and ready to meet his dad, he had already moved on to some responsibilities. We were disappointed, but we hoped we might run into him before we had to leave.

Tom's Story

The next morning, as Steve was on his way to check out from the motel, he saw Randy's dad, Tom, having breakfast. Steve introduced himself and asked if he could visit for a short while. Tom smiled and welcomed Steve to sit down.

Steve told him about our conversation with Randy and how impressed we were with him. From our brief time of discussion, Randy had really seemed to be a godly young man of character who enjoyed his family and working. Was this really the case? How long had Randy been like this? What were these parents doing to have their son's heart?

When he answered, Randy's dad shocked Steve. Just four years ago, Randy had been a very angry boy. Even those outside the family who knew him were well aware of his problem with anger. Over the last four years, God had done a mighty work in Randy's life. He wasn't perfect, but he was a young man who dearly loved his God and his family, enjoyed working, and has had victory over his anger.

Steve asked Tom how the Lord had worked in Randy's life. It actually began with Tom. Tom's focus changed to his family (Luke 1:17), whereas before it had been on himself. The principle that the family began applying about how they spent their time (aside from Tom's job) became, "If we can't do it as a family, we won't do it."

Tom said his golf clubs have about four years of dust on them now. He loved to golf and did quite well in tournaments. Some encouraged him that they could golf as a family, but he knew the passion would be rekindled. It wasn't worth pulling his heart away from his family again.

We expect that Tom's family was a very typical "religious" family. The children were in private school and in the normal activities. In addition, like his friends, Randy was on basketball and baseball teams.

However, God started working in Randy's parents' lives. They decided to homeschool the children. Seeking solutions to Randy's anger, they made changes to help their son. The parents continued to be obedient to the Lord's leading and, over the past four years, have seen God do a mighty work in their family.

These parents responded to the Lord's direction and have spiritual fruit as a result. Tom is quick to say they aren't perfect and still have some consequences from their earlier lifestyle, but the change is welcome and continuing.

Where Is My Heart?

Tom's home is a wonderful example of Malachi 4:6, "And he shall turn the heart of the fathers to the children, and the heart of the children to their fathers, lest I come and smite the earth with a curse." The futures of many children could be positively changed if only the parents' hearts would be turned toward their children.

Malachi 4:6 is critical to relationship building with children and to keeping their hearts. We tend to think a father and mother's heart is automatically focused on their children when, in reality, it isn't. That is why the Lord used the word "turn." The emphasis is on changing direction, from bad to good. The Hebrew word for turn is the twelfth most frequently used verb in the Old Testament. Just as we must repent and turn our hearts to God, we must renew our focus on our children.

It seems that the parent often thinks a troubled situation is his child's problem. "He just won't listen to me." "I've told him a hundred times, and he won't obey me." However, in our home, we have seen that it all begins with dad and mom's hearts. Have we turned our hearts toward the children?

We questioned Tom concerning what he would have said had someone asked him years ago if his heart was turned toward his children. His response was that he wouldn't have known what they meant. We then pursued with whether or not he had his own activities and the children had theirs? He said, "Yes, that was true."

We wonder if many dads and moms think their hearts are turned toward their children, when in fact they aren't. What has your heart? Next to the Lord, where is your mental and emotional focus? If your answer is your children, do a reality check on that. Aside from dad's work time or mom's daily responsibilities, how do you spend your time?

Our Treasure

"Lay not up for yourselves treasures upon earth, where moth and rust doth corrupt, and where thieves break through and steal: But lay up for yourselves treasures in heaven, where neither moth nor rust doth corrupt, and where thieves do not break through nor steal: For where your treasure is, there will your heart be also" (Matthew 6:19-21). In context, this verse is talking about laying up treasure in heaven, but we could apply the truth contained here to the parent-and-child relationship. If we take what we value – our time and effort – and invest it in our children, then our hearts will be turned to them. Face it. There are a myriad of important, urgent, or fun things that can take every minute we have. Then we toss our children the scraps of time that are left over, when we should be doing the opposite.

Sitting on Steve's desk in front of him is a "gold brick" with the words "Outstanding Performance" engraved on top. He was awarded this treasure in 1983 for his many hours of "meritorious" work at his corporate job. His gold brick has become very meaningful to him but not, perhaps, in the way you might think. The brick is actually solid brass, even though it has the look and feel of gold. Funny what a striking analogy it is, being as deceptive in its true value as his hours to earn it were deceptive in their true, eternal value.

For Steve, his brick has become a symbol of how his normal daily work is about as worthless as that fake "gold brick." It has become a frequent reminder of how easy it is to have misplaced priorities. When it comes to eternity, the hours men spend at work are comparatively wood, hay, and stubble. "For other foundation can no man lay than that is laid, which is Jesus Christ. Now if any man build upon this foundation gold, silver, precious stones, wood, hay, stubble; Every man's work shall be made manifest: for the day shall declare it, because it shall be revealed by fire; and the fire shall try every man's work of what sort it is. If any man's work abide which he hath built thereupon, he shall receive a reward. If any man's work shall be burned, he shall suffer loss: but he himself shall be saved; yet so as by fire" (1 Corinthians 3:11-15).

Just think, for many men with secular jobs, the work they spend eight or more hours a day doing is all going to be consumed in eternity. This work, which becomes most men's identity, will burn. It won't even give off bright colors and fancy sparks that dazzle the eye like we see on the Fourth of July. The flames will simply devour all their precious effort, and nothing will be left of eternal value as they stare at the ashes. Of course, it is a man's responsibility to provide for his family, so the real work of eternal value can be carried forth. Plus the money a man earns can be used to further the Kingdom of God. In general, however, the work men spend so many hours a day doing will count for nothing in eternity.

How easy it is to be deceived into thinking important work occurs during the for-pay job, but the work done at home isn't as important. That is backwards! Finally, when a father comes home to his family, that is when he has the opportunity for gold, silver, and precious stones. The question is: Are you creating more wood, hay, and stubble when you come home, or is it gold, silver, and precious stones? We each have a choice with our hours at home with our families.

Right Priorities

Steve has come to realize that the time he spends with his family, leading them in the ways of the Lord Jesus, is when something of value is produced. Discipling his family for the few hours he has available is the primary investment he can make for something that will last for eternity. He feels that even if he were in the ministry full time rather than having a secular job, his time with his family would still be his opportunity to spend those minutes on something of the greatest value.

We have heard from some dads who believe they can't fulfill Deuteronomy 6 unless they are working from home. We would encourage any father who feels this way to question whether he is doing everything he can while in his current vocation. Is Dad spending the time he has at home focused on his family with an eye on his heart being turned toward his children? Is Dad having a personal time with the Lord each day that will grow him spiritually so he can lead his family? Is Dad gently coaxing each child to spend time daily with the Lord? Is Dad leading the family in Bible reading and worship each day in the home? Is Dad spending his discretionary time with his family? If not, we don't believe coming home to work is the answer.

Our Personal Time

It is very easy to allow ourselves to invest whatever free minutes we have each day in our personal, adult pursuits and to leave the children to their own devices. This is true even in families where mom is home all day, homeschooling, and where dad is there in the evenings. We can fall into a rut of thinking that because we are in the house, our hearts are turned toward our children. A good gauge to evaluate this would be to see what we do when we have some available time. Does Dad turn on the TV? Does Mom go to her favorite Internet message board or call a friend? Maybe Dad heads out alone to his shop while Mom pulls out her crafts.

If we want to keep our children's hearts, we are going to make different choices. Dad will make sure the television is banished from their home, and he will take his son to the shop with him to make a project. Mom will sit down and read to her children or perhaps play a game with them. If she has work to do, she can include her children in what she is doing.

Our children will be our priority. They will be part of work projects we need to accomplish. Teaching them and talking to them will hold precedence. Activities can be evaluated against where they will turn the hearts of both the parents and the children. These activities will often be joint ones rather than separate ones.

Mom's Home Business

Many Christian women have chosen not to work outside the home. They often feel, though, that they should be contributing to the family income. Dad may agree, so Mom finds a home business for her "spare" time.

While it may appear when this decision is made that Mom has time for a home business, the reality is often different. The business causes Mom to live under constant stress and time pressure. Business demands limit time for her higher priority of homeschooling her children. It can consume her thoughts and emotional energy. It can even threaten her health. Her heart is turned toward her business, rather than toward her children. Each family must carefully evaluate the impact a home business has on Mom and, in particular, her ability to turn her heart toward her children.

No Regrets

We cherish the years of raising our children, and we desire to have no regrets when we look back on these years. We delight in spending time with our children. However, this is a choice. We can easily be drawn to our own personal activities. Next to each other, our children are our best friends. The time we have with our children is treasure that does not rust and cannot be stolen.

Steve has a passion for flying private airplanes, and yet he hasn't flown for more than twenty years. He laid that use of time and money aside for something of far greater value – time with his children and a heart focused on them. So many things will creep in to steal away our time and attention!

A daddy and a mommy's heart focused on their children is an amazing thing. God used Tom's change of heart direction in a mighty way in Randy's life. The truth in Malachi is real. If we will turn our hearts toward our children, they will turn their hearts toward us. Families all around are experiencing awful consequences for not having hearts turned toward each other. Are you willing to turn your heart toward your children?

Questions

1. Is your heart turned toward your children?

   a. How is that demonstrated or not demonstrated in your life?

2. Where is your mental and emotional focus?

3. How do you spend your time?

4. If you have free time, do you spend any of it with your children?

5. Does Mom have a home business?

   a. If so, how does it affect where her heart is?

6. Is Dad making the most of the time he is home to demonstrate his heart is turned to his children?

7. If your heart isn't turned toward your children, what changes would need to happen to turn it toward them?

◆　◆　◆　◆　◆　◆　◆

I have not only been protected from outside influences, but I have also been protected from myself. As a result, I felt I became more fully prepared and equipped to enter the world to work and minister, as Christ would use me. Christopher

◆　◆　◆　◆　◆　◆　◆

Chapter 4

Directing Children's Hearts Goals and Appetites

A major thrust of keeping our children's hearts is knowing where we want to direct those hearts. If we have our child's heart, we then own the responsibility of what we do with it. What goals do we have for our children? What appetites are being developed in their lives by the choices we are making as we parent? Goals and appetites will have a tremendous impact on what we do with our children's hearts. In addition, these goals and appetites will, if they are biblical, be instrumental in the keeping of our children's hearts and then directing their hearts to the Lord Jesus (Romans 10:10).

We have spoken with parents who explain their children's wrong decisions based on the child's freedom of choice as he matures and is given greater liberty. In these discussions there usually is no mention of all the years the parents were making the decisions and shaping the life of the child. What were their goals? What did they allow their children to do and not to do? What appetites did the parents let grow in their children's lives when the parents were the ones making the decisions? "Train up a child in the way he should go: and when he is old he will not depart from it" (Proverbs 22:6). What we have done with our children's hearts has tremendous effect on whether their hearts are turned toward their God and toward their parents. It also greatly affects the independent decisions these children will make.

Specific Goals

Pastor Bill Anderson used to say regularly in his sermons when we were in his church, "Nothing becomes dynamic until it becomes specific." That dear man was encouraging his flock to make specific spiritual goals and strive to attain them. In the same way, without an idea of where we want to go with our children's hearts, why would we even care if we had their hearts?

Paul had a goal in mind. "Brethren, I count not myself to have apprehended: but *this* one thing *I do,* forgetting those things which are behind, and reaching forth unto those things which are before, I press toward the mark for the prize of the high calling of God in Christ Jesus" (Philippians 3:13-14). The word "mark" means goal, something off in the distance that is aimed for. It keeps one from getting lost. The person who has a goal ahead keeps his attention on that goal. If he is distracted and takes his focus off the goal, he will likely be sidetracked and miss the mark. As a parent, having biblical goals for your children enables you to know how to direct their hearts and which parenting decisions are consistent with your goals.

The Lord Jesus is our example, and He always had His goal before Him. "Looking unto Jesus the author and finisher of *our* faith; who for the joy that was set before him endured the cross, despising the shame, and is set down at the right hand of the throne of God" (Hebrews 12:2). Jesus continually had His eyes on the cross. He would not tolerate those things that were a distraction from His purpose. When Peter suggested that the cross should not be ahead for Jesus, he was rebuked sharply by Jesus because avoiding the cross would come between Him and His goal.

Goals Give Direction and Help Us Stay on Track

If we have goals for our children, we know where we are headed as parents. It allows everyone to see clearly what lies at the end of the path. Explanations for not doing one thing and choosing to do another reaffirm the goal. When biblical goals have been articulated to the family, they provide a basis for all decisions. Dad and Mom aren't seen as making selfish, arbitrary choices that just happen to suit how they feel at the moment. Not only does it make day-to-day decisions easier, but it also eliminates the need for many decisions, because one can quickly see that the issue is contrary to the family goals.

In order to keep the hearts of our children, we think it is very important for them to know where the family is headed, courtesy of our biblical goals. Picture airplane passengers seated before takeoff but not knowing where the plane is headed. Parents are far less likely to frustrate their children when the children know the direction.

In addition to keeping their hearts, we show our children respect when we tell them our goals for them. In one way, it brings them closer to our level. We see that Christ did this with the disciples. "Henceforth I call you not servants; for the servant knoweth not what his lord doeth: but I have called you friends; for all things that I have heard of my Father I have made known unto you" (John 15:15). Jesus shared what the Father had told Him, and when we share our God-given goals with our children, it serves to increase the heart bonds.

"For the Father loveth the Son, and sheweth him all things that himself doeth: and he will shew him greater works than these, that ye may marvel" (John 5:20). We can learn so much by observing the Father's relationship with the Son. Here we see that because of the Father's love for the Son, He shows the Son all that He does. A great way to demonstrate our love for our children is to share our goals with them. This in turn helps us keep their hearts.

Clear biblical goals keep our family on track. We have to admit that there have been a number of times when we made a decision that was not consistent with a previously announced family direction. Frankly, we just hadn't thought through the ramifications of that to which we were agreeing. Next thing we knew, though, someone in the family was asking whether we were changing to a different way. With the accountability of that innocent reminder, we were back on track, thanks to our family goals and the family members knowing those goals. For us, we have found biblical goals to be wonderful.

For example, one of our goals is to raise children who love God's Word and know how to apply it to their lives. That is one reason why our daily family altar time is so very important to us. However, life is busy, and there are a myriad of urgent things that desire to gobble up our time in the Word. Even when we may be spending a long day in the van traveling, it would be easy to let "just one day" be missed. However, we know that habits, whether good or bad ones, are begun one step at a time. Therefore, it is a rare day when we don't gather around God's Word, read it, and discuss it. The goal that our children love God's Word keeps us on track with our time investment to make our family Bible time a priority and a blessing to the children.

What Kind of Goals?

We wonder if one of the most effective ways of understanding a person's theology is by observing how he applies Scripture to his life. What a person truly believes, he will put into practice. Not only will it affect how he lives, but also we would expect to see it in his goals for raising his children For example, how serious are we about the commands of Scripture? Do we love His Word, embrace it, and want to live a life pleasing to Him? Are we constantly looking for the line of sin so we can live as close to the world as possible without sinning, or do we desire to draw as close to Jesus as we can? As you read our family goals later in this chapter, we hope you see a picture painted in them of how we desire to apply God's Word to our lives. What about your goals? What do they reflect?

If we want to keep our children's hearts, our goals will be rooted in God's Word. The primary goal would be that our children come to a saving knowledge of Jesus Christ (Romans 10:10). All of our other spiritual goals would then reflect Christian lives of love, obedience, and service. These are goals that will draw our children to Jesus Christ and allow us to keep their hearts.

Appetites

Paul, speaking by the inspiration of the Holy Spirit, understood the power of appetites. Paul was no ordinary man. He was a Spirit-filled apostle of the Lord Jesus Christ. Yet he knew that unless he kept his appetites under control, they might cause his ministry to be shipwrecked. "But I keep under my body, and bring *it* into subjection: lest that by any means, when I have preached to others, I myself should be a castaway" (1 Corinthians 9:27). If human appetites could cause Paul to lose his ministry, then we must acknowledge that appetites can affect us as well. Paul is saying that we have to come to grips with how enslaving appetites are.

Appetites can greatly affect whether we keep our children's hearts or lose them. Wrong appetites pull children's hearts from the Lord and from their parents. Positive appetites do the opposite. As we consider goals for our children and what influences we allow into their lives, we would be wise to consider the appetites each goal and influence may cultivate.

An Appetite Example

God created in us a physical appetite that draws a man and woman together. It is a powerful appetite that has been at the root of both countless tragedies and blissful marriages. The same God-given appetite is responsible for good and bad. It is good when confined within certain boundaries and bad when stirred before its time or misapplied.

"Therefore shall a man leave his father and his mother, and shall cleave unto his wife: and they shall be one flesh" (Genesis 2:24). At the right time and with the right person, adult children leaving home to begin their own family is a blessed and God-ordained event. Unfortunately, let two young people who are not emotionally, spiritually, and physically prepared for marriage "fall in love," and you have an age-old recipe for disaster. Needless to say, the couple no longer has their hearts turned toward their parents. They are not teachable but are now focused on pleasing themselves. The couple's appetites have "kicked in" while reason checks out. What sadness could have been averted if only parents would have understood the power of appetites?

In this case, if our goal is that our children would be pure at marriage, then we will be cautious about influences we allow into their lives that might stir up a sexual appetite before marriage. We used one of the most powerful examples of an appetite to set the stage as an introduction, but there are a host of other appetites for which we must be on guard. We are constantly vigilant regarding appetites and their effect on our children – truly a difficult, continual task.

Good and Bad Appetites

For this book we will define an appetite as the emotion people feel when they set their affection on something they desire and want to incorporate more of it in their life. It is easy to see that the definition can apply to a host of things in our lives. It is possible the same appetite may be good or bad, depending on how it is used. Consider eating: most everyone has certain foods that he really likes. If a person's appetite for those foods were left unrestrained, it would be sinful, and there would be negative consequences. However, in general, a desire to eat is a good appetite. It keeps the body nourished.

As parents, we eliminate as many influences as we can that will possibly develop wrong appetites. In addition, because not every negative appetite comes from an outside influence, we teach our children how to have self-control through their years in our home.

When the Maxwell men go to the homeless mission each month, we see the effects of drugs and alcohol on the lives of many. We think few would argue that an appetite for drugs and alcohol can be disastrous. Therefore, they are something that we desire our family would avoid like the plague. Some other appetites that the Maxwells would consider negative are sports, Internet surfing, movies, television, and smoking.

There are spiritual appetites that we want for our children such as praying, hunger for the Word, and sharing Jesus Christ with others. These are positive and beneficial appetites that help us keep our children's hearts. Other spiritual appetites that we choose to encourage are love for the Lord Jesus Christ, preaching, contentment, gratitude, fellowship with other believers, serving others, and obedience to the Word.

By now it shouldn't surprise you if we say our desire is that our biblical goals would become our children's appetites. That is why we need to make sure that the Lord directs those goals. We are responsible to the Lord for how we raise these children (Ephesians 6:4), and it is not our option to raise them in any fashion we choose. For what do you want your children to have an appetite? They are wise parents who will consider the power of appetites as they develop goals for their children.

Developing Goals

What if you don't have any goals at this point? We would suggest you take the time to prayerfully establish some. This section will lead you step by step as you develop biblical goals for your family and children. Since God has a unique purpose for each family (Jeremiah 1:5), we aren't telling you what your goals should be. Each parent will stand before the Lord Jesus someday and have to give an account. It will not be acceptable to say, "Lord, I was following the Maxwells' goals for my children." It is possible our goals might be the same. However, it is important that you develop your own goals as the Lord directs.

Step 1: The only way to set down biblical, God-given goals is by looking to the Bible and praying. Then double-check what you believe the Lord to be telling you against His written Word. The two will never contradict each other. If we build our lives upon God's Word, then we will be like the man who built his house on the rock. Otherwise we are building our house on sand (Matthew 7:24-27).

Step 2: Note any specific Scriptures that you want to reflect in your goals.

Step 3: Consider what appetite will be developed in your children by each goal.

Step 4: Write down the goals and the reference for each one.

Step 5: Put your goals up where you will see them frequently. They are a great reminder of what you are to do each day. (Ours hang in the bathroom, next to the mirror, where we see them while we brush our teeth.)

Step 6: Share the goals with your children.

Step 7: Evaluate your goals periodically. Realize that these goals will likely be refined over time, as you grow closer to the Lord.

Step 8: Rate each child on every goal regularly. How are they doing? Is there progress, or is more attention needed?

Our Family's Goals

We have chosen to share some of our family goals as an example. Reading a family's goals will give you a good snapshot of where the family wants to go. You likely will have some goals that are similar to ours and some that are different.

Maxwells' Family Goals

Each member of the family would have a saving knowledge of the Lord Jesus Christ and serve Him (John 3:16, Hebrews 9:14) and:

1. joyfully serve others (Galatians 5:13, Colossians 3:17, Romans 12:1)

2. be obedient (John 14:15)

3. respect others (Romans 12:10)

4. be self-disciplined (Galatians 5:23)

5. love children (Matthew 19:14)

6. pursue holiness (Romans 12:1, Titus 1:8, 1 Peter 1:15,16)

7. court and not date (Romans 12:1)

8. live as ambassadors for Christ, including:

    a. speaking, writing, and dressing appropriately (Colossians 3:17)

    b. learning to edify rather than criticize (Romans 14:19, 1 Thessalonians 5:11)

    c. being content (Philippians 4:11)

9. love His Word, have a good understanding of the Bible and church doctrine (2 Timothy 2:15)

10. give their hearts to us as long as they are living in our home (Proverbs 23:26)

A major facet of keeping our children's hearts is knowing where we want to direct those hearts. What kinds of goals do we have for our children? What appetites are being developed in their lives by the choices we are making as we parent? Goals and appetites will have a tremendous impact first on our ability to keep our children's hearts, and then on what we do with their hearts. As we direct our children in these goals, can you see how they would help us keep their hearts? Each one is directly related to Scripture and protects from negative outside influences.

It would be greatly beneficial if you would take the time right now to write down your biblical goals for your children. There is something about having them right in front of you, documented on paper, that makes them more real. Having your goals written down will be useful to you as you continue to read.

Have We Considered Our Goals and Appetites?

Goals are an important part of raising a family. Even though most families have not taken time to write them down, we hope that you now have done that and will realize the benefits of doing so. Goals can play a crucial role in keeping your children's hearts. They define to your family "where God is calling you to go." Your goals based on God's Word should be a framework for decisions that are made regarding the children. *"In every step you take about them, in every plan, and scheme, and arrangement that concerns them, do not leave out that mighty question, 'How will this affect their souls?'" (J. C. Ryle).*

Can parents go wrong by keeping a close eye on what appetites are being created in their children's lives and how those appetites will affect their children's hearts? We have read many an e-mail from a brokenhearted parent who lost his child's heart because an appetite pulled the child's heart away.

Prayerfully consider whether you are on track with your goals for your children. If you have drifted, make the corrections now before it is too late, and you have lost your child's heart. Goals and appetites are powerful and must be handled with care as you strive to keep your children's hearts and direct them according to God's leading.

Questions

1. Have you written down biblical goals for your children?

   a. Write the reference next to each goal.

2. What appetites do you see in your children's lives?

   a. Which ones are positive?

   b. Which ones are negative?

   c. What have you allowed in your children's lives that have developed these appetites – both positive ones and negative ones?

   d. What changes could you make to eliminate negative appetites?

   e. What changes could you make to build positive appetites?

◆　◆　◆　◆　◆　◆　◆

God hasn't blessed my wife and me with children yet, but when He does, I want them to know that I'm in fellowship with the Lord. Nathan

◆　◆　◆　◆　◆　◆　◆

Chapter 5

The Foundation for Keeping Hearts

There is a very basic starting place for keeping our children's hearts. It is time in the Word and prayer. This key ingredient for the keeping of hearts is something that we, as parents, can greatly influence as our children are growing up in our homes.

Individual spiritual feeding for Dad, Mom, and each child old enough to read, through daily Bible reading and prayer, is vital if we are to keep our children's hearts. In addition, spending time reading and discussing the Bible as a family is also critical. Consider how every spiritual goal we have for our children should be based on God's Word. The foundation then must be laid in a love of, knowledge of, and understanding of the Bible. As the Bible is discussed, the Spirit of God will speak to the children, affirming the direction of the family.

Imagine the difficulty in keeping the hearts of your children if they spoke a different language from you as parents. Would it even be possible? That is a picture of the problem when some in the family are in the Bible daily and others aren't. They don't all have the same frame of reference, so keeping children's hearts becomes that much more difficult.

Does It Matter?

Steve once had a very engaging discussion for about an hour with a young man in his early teens. The boy was strongly opinionated, and Steve enjoyed asking him questions as he tried to understand what the basis was for the vocational decisions this teen was making. The young man was intelligent and articulate, and yet as they talked, it was obvious to Steve that there was a major flaw in the boy's reasoning. His goals and how he was spending his time did not match up with the biblical values he espoused.

Steve then asked the teen about personal and family devotions. He said he was having individual time with the Lord, but his family didn't read Scripture together. After hearing himself and realizing how it might sound to Steve, he thought for a moment and said, "Well, I guess I'd have to say that our family devotion is sort of all day. It is the way we live."

While "devotional living" is great, it doesn't take the place of reading and studying our Bibles and entering our prayer closets (Matthew 6:6). We want to help direct our children in their understanding of Scripture and its personal application. This may happen in a hit-or-miss fashion with devotional living. However, daily family Bible time ensures that we are studying God's Word thoroughly throughout the years our children are in our homes and learning to apply Scripture to their lives.

Feed My Sheep

There is a wonderful, elderly man we know at the nursing home, and we love him dearly. We have known him for close to ten years, but we're afraid he won't live much longer. The biggest problem seems to be that he doesn't eat and, therefore, is wasting away. We don't see how such a thin person can continue to lose weight. The food seems to be good, but we're told he just sits, picks at it for a while, and then quits. He will die without nourishment. Without spiritual nourishment, our children, too, will waste away spiritually.

Have you ever thought about the fact that God did not have to make our bodies to need food? However, He had a purpose in it. "Give us day by day our daily bread" (Luke 11:3). We require continued sustenance to keep our focus on our Provider.

The reality of physical food is used by the Lord to teach us about our need for spiritual food. In John 21:15-17 we read, "So when they had dined, Jesus saith to Simon Peter, Simon, *son* of Jonas, lovest thou me more than these? He saith unto him, Yea, Lord; thou knowest that I love thee. He saith unto him, Feed my lambs. He saith to him again the second time, Simon, *son* of Jonas, lovest thou me? He saith unto him, Yea, Lord; thou knowest that I love thee. He saith unto him, Feed my sheep. He saith unto him the third time, Simon, *son* of Jonas, lovest thou me? Peter was grieved because he said unto him the third time, Lovest thou me? And he said unto him, Lord, thou knowest all things; thou knowest that I love thee. Jesus saith unto him, Feed my sheep." Jesus was not talking about Simon Peter physically feeding sheep but rather spiritually feeding the flock.

Notice how Jesus related Peter's love for Christ with Peter's feeding those for whom he would soon be responsible. Peter would be leader of the church in Jerusalem, and if Peter loved Jesus, Peter was to feed them spiritually. In asking the question three times with slight variations, Jesus was making His point very clear. "Peter, if you love Me, you will feed My sheep." That is true of parents, especially dads, as well. If we love the Lord Jesus, we will spiritually feed those He has entrusted to our care.

Spiritual Food and the Shepherd

In John 10:3-4 we read, "To him the porter openeth; and the sheep hear his voice: and he calleth his own sheep by name, and leadeth them out. And when he putteth forth his own sheep, he goeth before them, and the sheep follow him: for they know his voice." The shepherd leads the sheep out to find good pasture. He is careful that the sheep only eat what is beneficial for them, avoiding what is harmful. He cares about the sheep and wants to see them grow and be healthy. A shepherd may be negligent in several areas and still not devastate the flock, but if he is not feeding them, they will be hurt. That applies to our families. We may fail our families in many ways, but if we aren't feeding them spiritually every day, they will greatly suffer.

In Ezekiel 34, God is amazing as He blasts those shepherding Israel. ". . . Woe *be* to the shepherds of Israel that do feed themselves! should not the shepherds feed the flocks? Ye eat the fat, and ye clothe you with the wool, ye kill them that are fed: *but* ye feed not the flock" (Ezekiel 34:2-3). "Thus saith the Lord GOD; Behold, I *am* against the shepherds; and I will require my flock at their hand, and cause them to cease from feeding the flock . . ." (Ezekiel 34:10). God harshly judges the shepherds who will not nurture their sheep.

Can we be serious about our desire to raise children who will be men and women of God without feeding them the spiritual food that they will need to grow spiritually strong and healthy? Can we hope to keep their hearts if they aren't grounded in the Word? How can they resist the world if they are not spiritually mighty?

A homeowner who says he is working hard to grow a nice, healthy lawn and never feeds it is only fooling himself. All his neighbors know the truth merely by observing his lawn and what steps he is taking. They can see that his actions aren't consistent with his words. In the same way, those around us who observe our children and who visit our home will soon come to understand what emphasis we place on spiritually feeding our family.

What Scripture Says

Consider these verses in Proverbs and how they suggest that if we want to keep our children's hearts, we will ground them daily in the Word of God. "My son, if thou wilt receive my words, and hide my commandments with thee; So that thou incline thine ear unto wisdom, *and* apply thine heart to understanding; Yea, if thou criest after knowledge, *and* liftest up thy voice for understanding; If thou seekest her as silver, and searchest for her as *for* hid treasures; Then shalt thou understand the fear of the LORD, and find the knowledge of God. For the LORD giveth wisdom: out of his mouth *cometh* knowledge and understanding. He layeth up sound wisdom for the righteous: *he is* a buckler to them that walk uprightly. He keepeth the paths of judgment, and preserveth the way of his saints. Then shalt thou understand righteousness, and judgment, and equity; *yea,* every good path" (Proverbs 2:1-9). "All scripture *is* given by inspiration of God, and *is* profitable for doctrine, for reproof, for correction, for instruction in righteousness: That the man of God may be perfect, thoroughly furnished unto all good works" (2 Timothy 3:16-17).

This is only a sampling of the verses we can find in Scripture that will encourage us to build Scripture into our children's lives. It is abundantly clear that God's Word is the basis for every aspect of our lives. It will be foundational in the quest to keep our children's hearts.

Sometimes we have wondered whether the reason we have kept our children's hearts is partially because they have been so well grounded in the Word. Psalm 119:11 says, "Thy word have I hid in mine heart, that I might not sin against thee." Psalm 119:105 continues, "Thy word *is* a lamp unto my feet, and a light unto my path." Our children spent personal time in the Word, family time in the Word, and school time in the Word. Could it be that God's Word was so ingrained in their thoughts and lives that it became their standard and direction? While they obviously had their own sin natures to deal with, they also had the truths of Scripture strongly embedded in their hearts to battle the pull of the world.

Where Is Dad's Heart?

It is not uncommon for us to hear a dad say that he greatly desires to have family Bible time because he knows how important it is. He will, though, sigh and continue to explain how busy the family is and how seldom they are at home in the evenings. This dad is showing his true priorities. If outside activities cause a family to skip their Bible time, then, bluntly put, the outside activities need to go.

We have heard parents who have lost their child's heart say they did everything they could to teach him the ways of the Lord and ground him in his faith. However, when questioned about family Bible time, one discovers this family did not have much, if any at all, family Bible reading.

Spiritually feeding those for whom we are responsible is critical in keeping hearts. Just as there are repercussions from the government if parents don't physically feed their children, there are consequences when parents don't spiritually feed their children. Why is it so many dads don't lead their family in daily Bible reading when this is so serious? There are probably a myriad of answers, but none of them matter.

We believe if dads realized the consequences they would experience and observe in the lives of their children for not spiritually feeding them, they would get serious, and excited, about daily feeding their family God's Word.

A friend of ours told us about his childhood. His family had a daily family altar of Bible reading. However, he said it was obvious that his father had little spiritual interest in the Bible time, even though he led it. As a result, the family picked up on Dad's attitude about spiritual matters, and in time the whole family was spiritually shipwrecked. Studying God's Word as a family is not a silver bullet or something to be checked off on a checklist. Daily fellowshipping together around the Bible is very important, but Dad's heart must be in it.

Do we make our daily family devotion time appetizing? Does our family look forward to dining on God's Word together? Does the family see our enthusiasm for digging out jewels in Scripture? Is it something we are excited about like a hungry person with a steak dinner, or do we force ourselves to take a few bites? If we aren't interested in God's Word, then we need not expect our families to be excited.

Family Bible and Prayer Time

"Our daughter is five. We have begun including her in our family Bible time, but we feel like we waited too long. We are now playing catchup." A dad with young children

We encourage you to have all of your children in your family Bible time, even babies. Please don't water down God's Word by using Bible storybooks for younger children.

Begin from their earliest days giving them an interest in and hunger for God's Word. Let them see that it applies even to the two-year-old who is struggling with saying "no" to Mommy or who is not sharing toys.

When Steve started leading the family devotion, he felt Teri could have done a far better job. That was okay, though, because he knew he needed to do it, and God would enable him to improve over time. The Lord has been faithful through the years in teaching Steve how to lead his family's Bible time. He will do the same for you if you will begin. So, Dad, what are you feeding your family tonight?

We also have seen the importance of praying with our children. Our family does this at bedtime. Steve puts the younger boys to bed, and Teri the girls. Each person prays out loud. This allows the children to hear their parents pray and to learn from it. In addition to the benefits of the actual praying, it helps make the children more comfortable in spoken prayer.

Personal Bible Time

We want to spiritually feed our children through daily family Bible reading and discussion, which helps us keep their hearts. In addition, we should be encouraging them to spend time each day reading their Bibles and praying alone. This would start when they have become proficient readers. As parents, we can motivate our children to read their Bibles. We do this by first setting the example in our own lives and spending time alone with the Lord each day in Bible reading and prayer.

We can help our child set aside a time to spend with the Lord personally every day. As our children reached an age when they read well enough to start consistently having their own daily Bible time, Teri put this as an activity planned into their schedule.

We motivate the children to have their personal Bible time by planning to purchase each one his own nice study Bible and cover after he has had daily, personal Bible reading and prayer for six months. The children know this reward is before them and eagerly anticipate picking out their Bible and cover.

Dad or Mom should give children direction in selecting books of the Bible to read through. This helps the child with some specifics when faced with a book to read as big as the Bible. Asking children questions about what they are reading is beneficial as well.

The Only Sure Foundation

The only sure foundation for raising sons and daughters who walk with the Lord Jesus Christ without rebellion or immorality is to make the Bible important every day in the home. *"But if you love your children, let the simple Bible be everything in the training of their souls"* (J. C. Ryle). The Bible has to be read and studied by each parent so that they are maintaining an intimate, meaningful relationship with the Lord. The Bible should be read in a family setting with Dad leading this daily time.

We want to bring our children to a place where they will read their Bibles and pray alone every day so that they will be able to personally learn about Jesus and what He wants for their lives. Time in the Word by each family member keeps everyone's frame of reference on a biblical foundation. Scripture will remind your children why you have chosen the goals you have. It puts God as the One setting the direction for the family. What is your foundation for keeping your children's hearts? Have you built upon the Rock and only the Rock?

Questions

1. Do Dad and Mom have consistent personal Bible and prayer times?

2. Does your family have family Bible time?

   a. Does Dad lead this time?

   b. How often do you have family Bible time?

   c. Do both Dad and Mom have their hearts in family Bible time?

3. Are there hindrances to family Bible time that need to be eliminated?

4. Does your family have prayer time?

5. Are your children having consistent personal Bible and prayer times?

   a. If not, what can you do to help them begin?

♦ ♦ ♦ ♦ ♦ ♦ ♦

I think one key to keeping my heart was my parents making sure they had an open line of communication with me at all times. Sarah

♦ ♦ ♦ ♦ ♦ ♦ ♦

Chapter 6

Building Parent-Child Relationships

Keeping the heart of a child involves maintaining a close, loving, open relationship with him while being zealous of not tearing down that relationship through our anger, harshness, or bitterness (Ephesians 6:4). From what we have observed in our home and in others' relationships, we feel that anger and harshness are the greatest forces that drive a child's heart away from his parents. Our children must be bathed in love and acceptance.

In a way, this is a mini-reflection of our relationship with the Father. The blood of Jesus enables us to enter into a heart relationship with the Father. When we are born again (John 3), we become the children of God (John 1:12-13). Notice how God uses "family" terms so we will understand heavenly truths.

This is a beautiful picture of how ideally our relationship should be with our children. In the Bible, we see a God Who loves His children so much He died (through Christ) for them (John 3:16). The Father desires fellowship with His children more than anything. He wants to spend time with them, listen to them, teach them, and guide them. In return, He wants our hearts because He loves us and desires fellowship with us. Also, when He has our hearts, we are far less likely to be drawn away by the idols of this world. "Jesus said unto him, Thou shalt love the Lord thy God with all thy heart, and with all thy soul, and with all thy mind" (Matthew 22:37). The more we give Him our hearts, the more wonderful that relationship becomes.

This is true for the parent-child relationship as well. As parents, we are called to sacrifice for our children. We are to love them, spend time with them, listen to them, teach them, and guide them. "And thou shalt teach them diligently unto thy children, and shalt talk of them when thou sittest in thine house, and when thou walkest by the way, and when thou liest down, and when thou risest up" (Deuteronomy 6:7).

We also would like our children's hearts so that we can turn those hearts to Jesus Christ. "For with the heart man believeth unto righteousness; and with the mouth confession is made unto salvation" (Romans 10:10). It may be tempting at times to be satisfied with mere outward conformity from our children, but we really want their hearts. When we have our child's heart, the older the child becomes, the sweeter the fellowship not only between parent and child, but also between the child and Jesus.

We want to investigate those aspects of relationships that are key in keeping a child's heart. In the course of our daily lives, we can make choices that show our children our hearts are turned toward them, so they will turn their hearts to us.

Love

While love may be assumed to be essential in a relationship that keeps a child's heart, we want to make sure we emphasize it. What we discovered in our parenting was that generally it was easy to love a child, but sometimes it required a choice on our part (1 Corinthians 13:4-7). When the child was struggling with wrong behaviors and bad attitudes – particularly when this was ongoing – our natural tendency was to pull away from that child. Instead we had to return love for his unkindness. It was important to reach out to the child with hugs, pats, and physical closeness. As parents, we needed to encourage each other in our loving the difficult child and abundantly expressing this love to him. If consequences were necessary, then we had to be very gentle, matter-of-fact, and patient while giving them. Nothing could be done in a spirit of anger or revenge.

If we are to keep our children's hearts, they must feel our love so strongly that there is never any doubt of it in their minds. They should know we love them when they are obedient and when they are disobedient, when they are happy and when they are sad, when they are diligent and when they are negligent – all the time. This will be expressed verbally and through physical closeness such as an arm around a shoulder, a good morning kiss, a smile when we see them, or a walk-by hug. Love is a major undergirding for keeping our children's hearts.

If we say we love our children, but all they hear from us is criticism and correction, they probably won't feel that love. Our love has to be evident to them in a way they can understand. Whoever they feel loves them the most will have their heart. "For where your treasure is, there will your heart be also" (Matthew 6:21). As we invest our treasure of love in our children, our hearts will be with them. They must believe in our love for them if we want to keep their hearts.

Time – The Bottom Line

Why is it that more parents aren't concerned about keeping their children's hearts? First, we think many would say that they do want to keep their children's hearts. Unfortunately, there seems to be a disconnect. It is impossible for a father and mother to spend the majority of their time and mental focus on activities of their own personal interest and still have anything left for their children. There is no substitute for time. We are lying to ourselves if we think we can just spend quality time with the children, because we aren't willing to give quantity, and still be able to maintain a heart-keeping relationship. It takes time and effort to build the kind of relationship that keeps a child's heart. Investing that time is essential.

Relationships do not develop if we are not spending time together. The parent who wants to keep his child's heart will find it necessary to make that child a priority in his life. This will be evident by the time the parents spend with their children. It is very easy for parents to let other "good" activities steal their time. After all, time spent with our children isn't always the most exciting or enjoyable use of time. However, it is likely the most "eternal" use of our time.

Who's Going?

One-on-one time with our children has been important to us. Keeping hearts is reliant on strong, loving relationships. Those relationships are, in large measure, determined by the amount of time we spend together.

We remember vividly a season in our marriage when everything one of us did irritated the other. The feelings were equally negative between us. While this wasn't the way we wanted our relationship to continue, nothing was changing it.

One Saturday, we had a function to attend that required us to travel several hours in the car alone with each other. In the course of the extended time of our talking, the Lord re-knit our hearts to one another. It works the same way with our children.

Even if we have plenty of family time together, if we want to have our children's hearts, we will make individual time for each one. Teri did this by scheduling a half an hour into her afternoons that she would spend with one particular child each day. The children knew which day included their time with Mom and looked forward to it. In addition, Teri scheduled one child at a time to be a meal helper. This gave her necessary help with meal preparation, and it also enabled her the one-on-one talking time she wanted with every child on an ongoing basis.

Steve uses errand time to build relationships with the children. Often he will take one child with him when he has an outing to Kansas City, about forty-five minutes away. This allows a good amount of father-and-child talking time, plus going with Daddy is always a prized invitation.

Steve has been the grocery shopper in our family for more than fifteen years now. He would take as many of the children as were available, and for years that meant a baby in a backpack. Often there were six children with him, and they would all have a delightful time. What fun they would have as they fellowshipped together with a purpose. Steve wouldn't trade all the G-rated movies in the world for those shopping trips with his children.

In addition, work projects for Steve and our children were often done not simply to accomplish the job – Steve could have done it better himself – but so the children could learn skills and have the benefit of strong relationships with their dad. Working gave Steve and the children usefulness for their time together. It knit their hearts to each other as they worked and talked. We look for every opportunity to be with our children. Isn't that the way it is with best friends? Then isn't that the way it should be with our children?

Mother-Daughter Outings

While Teri and Sarah, our oldest daughter, had occasional excursions together, it was not on the regular, consistent basis Teri wanted. She always had good intentions of going out with Sarah. However, in reality, time slipped away with no "feet" being given to the intentions. Teri found that when evening came, she didn't have the energy left to take Sarah out unless she had planned it ahead of time.

When Sarah was about fourteen years old, she and Teri began going out to eat together on the first Monday of the month. They both look forward to this special time. Occasionally, Sarah invited one or both of her younger sisters to join them. Generally, though, this was an evening for just Sarah and Mom. Sarah would often bring up areas she was struggling with in her personal life. She and Teri could discuss those issues and find biblical ways to deal with them. She felt the freedom to ask questions and bring up topics she might not have been comfortable talking about at home where little ears were always about.

During their evenings out, they talked with each other, relaxed, and enjoyed the freedom of not making or cleaning up dinner. Teri planned a simple meal for the family at home that Steve and the children could easily make. Teri and Sarah were even a bit practical by running errands after they ate. Both Teri and Sarah have fond memories of their relationship-building outings, which still continue at the time of this writing!

Time Apart

Spending time apart is how relationships become distant. If we are physically and emotionally away from our children, we should expect their hearts not to be close to us. Sleeping in the same house is no more justification for our children's hearts being drawn to us than it is for people in an apartment building to have hearts drawn toward each other. There might be some degree of camaraderie because of proximity, but it is not a true drawing of hearts.

When Dad spends his time focused on everything but the children, his children are going to find someone who values them and wants to spend time with them. It matters little what Dad is spending his time doing. It could be long hours working. It could be hunting and fishing. It could be sports. It could even be something "worthwhile" such as being an elder at church. The bottom line is that children need their father. If Dad's heart isn't turned toward his children, as evidenced by how he spends his time, we shouldn't be surprised if they find someone else to whom they will give their hearts.

Even if Mom homeschools her children but her heart and interests are outside of the home, the children are likely going to pick up a similar outward focus. If Mom spends all her free time pursuing her personal interests or even ministries, can you see how she is facilitating passing her child's heart on to others?

Even if Dad and Mom are not physically separated from the children, if their hearts are separated emotionally, then the children will turn their hearts elsewhere. The Lord uses separation to move hearts. We need to understand that as parents if we sow "separation," we will reap someone else winning our children's hearts. "Be not deceived; God is not mocked: for whatsoever a man soweth, that shall he also reap. For he that soweth to his flesh shall of the flesh reap corruption; but he that soweth to the Spirit shall of the Spirit reap life everlasting" (Galatians 6:7-8).

For example, if we send our children away to Christian camps, seminars, or other educational opportunities, we can expect their hearts to be drawn elsewhere. There are lots of wonderful-sounding educational and ministry opportunities and experiences for our children away from home. Many families eagerly anticipate their children being old enough to be sent out to participate in these great learning or serving events. The focus is on what the child will experience and learn while he is away from home.

Unfortunately, it is not uncommon for this to begin the process of prematurely separating a child's heart from his parents. Some call it an independent spirit in the child. Others describe it as the child having some trouble adjusting to being back home again. Simply put, the parent is starting to lose, or has lost, the child's heart. Likely there will be little or no further discipling in that child's life by the parents without great effort being expended to draw the heart back.

We made this mistake with Nathan when he was seventeen. We allowed him to spend the summer away from us. There was a training program in another state that sounded wonderful. He wanted to go, and we "knew" it would be great for him. It involved other homeschooled children plus the opportunity for Nathan to minister in addition to learning. After being away from home for six weeks, as the time approached for Nathan to come home, he was pleading to be able to stay longer. We wished we had known before agreeing to the trip what we know now.

We would describe our relationship with Nathan after the trip as good. However, as all of us look back – Nathan included – we acknowledge that it wasn't the same after the trip as it was before. We want God's best for our family; even "good" isn't enough.

Smiling

It is vital that we smile at our children. We should do this when we talk to them or when we simply see them down the hall or across the room. Our smiles must communicate our pleasure to be in their company rather than showing annoyance at being interrupted or being required to listen to a long, childish tale. For some, smiling will come very naturally, but for others, it will be a purposed, learned behavior.

While a discussion of smiling at our children may seem very basic and unnecessary in the realm of relationships and keeping hearts, we encourage you to "watch" yourself for a day. How often does a smile light up your face when your child approaches you? When you are talking to your children, are you smiling? As they tell you something important to them, is your face beaming with a smile? Have you conveyed to your children, via your facial expressions, that your heart is fully turned toward them and committed to them? It is possible for us to think we are smiling at our children when in fact it happens only occasionally. In our desire to keep our children's hearts, may a starting place be the simplicity of a smile.

Praise

As parents with goals for our children of being godly men and women, we are usually very aware of their shortcomings. Our whole focus can become what they need to do to improve rather than what they have already accomplished. Proverbs reminds us of the importance of our words as we interact with our children: "The wise in heart shall be called prudent: and the sweetness of the lips increaseth learning" (Proverbs 16:21).

"A word fitly spoken *is like* apples of gold in pictures of silver. As an earring of gold, and an ornament of fine gold, *so is* a wise reprover upon an obedient ear" (Proverbs 25:11-12). Here we see how our words of praise and encouragement are to those who receive them. We also are made aware that there is a way to be a wise reprover, when a reproof is necessary.

If we want to keep our children's hearts, they must feel they are valued in our eyes. While this love and value may intrinsically be a part of our lives, we have to convey it to our children so that they are heedful of it. If all we ever do is to correct, rebuke, lecture, and discipline our children, it will be difficult for them to be aware of the love we have for them. However, if we continually find ways to praise, edify, and encourage them, their hearts will be pulled toward us. "We love him, because he first loved us" (1 John 4:19).

"Let no corrupt communication proceed out of your mouth, but that which is good to the use of edifying, that it may minister grace unto the hearers" (Ephesians 4:29). Think about how we like to be praised. Which do we enjoy more from a spouse, encouragement or a correction? As parents, our desire is to edify and build up our children to strengthen them, drawing their hearts to the Lord and to us. Our children will benefit if we make it a habit to praise them.

Conversation

You might never guess what one of the strongest relationship builders in our family is. It is our evening Bible time. As soon as Daddy calls everyone for family devotions and we begin to gather, conversation excitedly breaks out from all corners of the living room. The amazing thing is that we eat dinner together where lively discussions occur as well. However, there is still much to be talked about between family members, and sometimes it is difficult to input a word amidst the flutter of chatter.

Steve has made it a practice to allow for this talking time before we begin our Bible reading. Knowing the benefit of sharing our thoughts, feelings, and activities with each other in keeping his children's hearts, he plans extra time into evening devotions. Steve wants the family's Bible reading gathering to be a warm, comfortable, uplifting, looked-forward-to time. Allowing for personal conversation to flow before we start our reading has been a key ingredient in this.

Forgiveness

We have found that asking forgiveness of our children when we have wronged them in some way is an essential part of building a relationship that will enable us to keep their hearts. "Therefore if thou bring thy gift to the altar, and there rememberest that thy brother hath ought against thee; Leave there thy gift before the altar, and go thy way; first be reconciled to thy brother, and then come and offer thy gift" (Matthew 5:23-24). For us, being reconciled involves asking forgiveness for whatever the offense might have been. We might not think of doing this in a parent-and-child relationship, but it would apply just as it would in any other relationship.

If we won't admit wrongdoing to our children, we run the risk of bitterness building in them. "Looking diligently lest any man fail of the grace of God; lest any root of bitterness springing up trouble *you,* and thereby many be defiled" (Hebrews 12:15). A child's heart that is bitter toward a parent will most likely not be turned to that parent. When we ask our child's forgiveness for lack of patience, not being attentive, being unkind, or any other sin we may have committed against him, we are facilitating keeping his heart. Asking forgiveness is not only being obedient to Scripture, but it is also vital to maintaining loving relationships. "Confess *your* faults one to another, and pray one for another, that ye may be healed . . ." (James 5:16).

Anger

Perhaps the one most damaging aspect to a parent-and-child relationship is a parent's anger. We cannot expect to have and keep our children's hearts if we are continually angry with them. Anger will destroy any relationship we hope to have with our children. We simply cannot stress enough how wrong anger is within a family and how it must not be allowed in a parent's life.

Scripture is strong in its condemnation of anger. "Let all bitterness, and wrath, and anger, and clamour, and evil speaking, be put away from you, with all malice: And be ye kind one to another, tenderhearted, forgiving one another, even as God for Christ's sake hath forgiven you" (Ephesians 4:31-32). "But now ye also put off all these; anger, wrath, malice, blasphemy, filthy communication out of your mouth" (Colossians 3:8). "And, ye fathers, provoke not your children to wrath: but bring them up in the nurture and admonition of the Lord" (Ephesians 6:4). "Wherefore, my beloved brethren, let every man be swift to hear, slow to speak, slow to wrath: For the wrath of man worketh not the righteousness of God" (James 1:19-20).

If anger, to any degree at all, is a problem in your home, we suggest you listen to Dr. S. M. Davis' teaching tape, called "Freedom from the Spirit of Anger" (see page 284). He presents clear biblical insights on anger and how to overcome it. This tape is something that we listen to in our home on a regular basis. In addition, we have a recorded workshop on anger called "Anger – Relationship Poison" (see page 280).

Importance of Relationships for Keeping Hearts

Scripture tells us the importance of a son giving his father his heart: "My son, give me thine heart, and let thine eyes observe my ways" (Proverbs 23:26). As parents, we want to facilitate rather than hinder this giving of a heart. As we focus on building relationships with our children, we allow them to most naturally give us their hearts.

It is easy to become wrapped up in our own lives and responsibilities. In the midst of this, we can let our relationships with our children become sidelined. After all, we live with them, see them each day, and talk to them frequently. However, we want to go way beyond the basics of living in the same home with our children. We want them to feel our love for them, our value for them, even our liking of them.

"Kindness, gentleness, long suffering, forbearance, patience, sympathy, a willingness to enter into childish troubles, a readiness to take part in childish joys, - these are the cords by which a child may be led most easily, - these are the clues you must follow if you would find the way to his heart." (J. C. Ryle)

Dads and Moms, make building a relationship that keeps your children's hearts one of your highest priorities. Years down the road you may well have deep remorse that you didn't invest what was necessary to grow a relationship that will win and hold your child's heart. There is no sacrifice too great. You will never regret it. May we be parents who know the significance of loving relationships with our children in keeping their hearts. Then may we invest what is necessary to build those relationships.

Questions

1. What would your children say if you asked them how they know you love them?

2. How much time do you spend with your children each week?

3. Do you take your children with you when you go places?

4. Do you include them in projects?

5. Do you have any regular, scheduled outings with your children?

6. Have you considered what time apart may do to your relationship with your children?

7. Are you frequently smiling at your children?

8. Do you praise them often?

   a. In what way do you praise your children?

9. Do you talk with your children?

10. Do you have a problem with anger?

    a. If so, what has been the effect on your family relationships?

◆　◆　◆　◆　◆　◆　◆

Dad had a weekly meeting with me each Sunday, and he still does. I feel free to share whatever struggles I am having and know that he will give me direction, encouragement, and sympathy. Sarah

◆　◆　◆　◆　◆　◆

Chapter 7

Practicing Discipleship

Discipleship is the process of making disciples of Christ. This is an important role for the parent in his child's life, and it will impact his keeping of his child's heart. Discipleship involves, to us, the purposeful work of teaching our children God's truth and His ways. It is also the facilitating of a personal, intimate relationship with the Lord. Our lives will be filled with discipleship in the many daily interactions that take place with our children. However, discipleship should also occur at times that are specifically designated for this spiritual input.

Many young people are not strong soldiers for Christ because they have not been adequately prepared. Parents have assumed that because the child grew up in a Christian home and went to church, his spiritual maturity matched his physical maturity. This is often not the case without our investment in the discipleship process.

We have already discussed the importance of building God's Word into our children's lives. This is done through their personal and family Bible reading plus weekly corporate worship. "Not forsaking the assembling of ourselves together, as the manner of some *is;* but exhorting *one another:* and so much the more, as ye see the day approaching" (Hebrews 10:25).

In addition to these ways of discipleship, we had two more that we felt were valuable and useful. We could easily observe that they were not only helpful in building disciples for Christ but also in the keeping of our children's hearts.

Weekly Father-and-Child Meetings

Years ago someone suggested to Steve that he have weekly meetings with each of our children. Over the twelve years he has had these kinds of meetings, they have become one of Steve's favorite times of the week. Steve continued to meet with Nathan up until the week before Nathan's wedding. At the conclusion of their last meeting, Nathan said he would like to have meetings with his children. For Steve, this was wonderful affirmation of the value of that time together.

One of the most important aspects of the meetings is consistency. Life is busy, and the urgent often crowds out the important. Therefore, Steve had to find a time he could set aside and protect. For our family, that is Sunday after church at noon. While lunch preparations are under way, Steve will begin his meetings. Generally, there is no particular order, but whoever is most available begins. However, there are times when a child will ask to be first because he has something pressing he wants to discuss.

Steve has most of his meetings in our bedroom. It could be any room, as long as people are not coming and going and there is the opportunity for private sharing. We have a big rocking chair that was Teri's great-grandfather's, and the children like to sit in it while Steve lays crossways on the bed. They are both comfortable, and it is very conducive to a time of sharing.

There is no agenda, except as the Lord leads the discussion. If there have been difficulties during the week, they are likely to be brought up. Steve desires to lay the application of Scripture on the children's minds in relation to the events of the week and their conduct (Ephesians 6:4). It is a time of "coming alongside" and sharing as a close friend with another.

Steve's authority as a parent is seldom exercised during this time, but it is simply understood. There is no finger waving as a situation is discussed, but strings of love tied between hearts are tugged in the needed direction. Having our children's hearts enables these meetings to be effective. They are powerful in the influence they can bring to bear and immensely helpful in keeping the children's hearts. A shepherd leads his sheep with his voice; weekly meetings are key in maintaining our children's responsiveness to the voice of their father.

Often Steve will ask how a child's quiet time is going. He asks what they are reading and whether the Lord is putting any particular area of need on their heart. It is important to us that our children's quiet time is a time of feeding on the Word – a time of sweetness, learning, and growing in intimacy with the Lord Jesus. Depending on their answer, Steve might suggest they read different books of the Bible. The children need to see that Steve places a very high priority on the quality of their time in the Word. He will do anything he can to facilitate it.

There are times when the children might want to participate in something that would not be good for them. Steve will explain how Scripture applies to the situation and discuss it with them. The goal is that, when confronted with the truth of God's Word, they would embrace the same position as we have. There have been occasions when it was difficult at first for a child to accept something, but over time he has come to see the wisdom in the path that we are taking.

For those times when Steve sensed a heart beginning to drift, the meetings were also very important. They would discuss troubling issues and deal with any bitterness that had begun to grow. "Follow peace with all *men,* and holiness, without which no man shall see the Lord: Looking diligently lest any man fail of the grace of God; lest any root of bitterness springing up trouble *you,* and thereby many be defiled" (Hebrews 12:14-15).

For our family, those weekly meetings are indispensable. They are key in keeping our children's hearts. They are strategic in allowing us to be leaders by influence rather than leaders by authority. We can't imagine raising children without them.

Studies – Discipleship Tools

Steve is studying a Christian book with his thirteen- and fourteen-year-old sons. This is an excellent way to disciple. He is slowly working through the book individually with each of them. They get together and informally discuss notes they have made from reading the book through the week. It has been a very beneficial time for all three of them. They have not only discussed the book, but have discovered it provides a springboard for talk about other areas of their Christian walk.

One way Teri set out to disciple our oldest daughter, Sarah, was by planning weekly time to study a Christian women's book together. Their study time was for half an hour, two nights a week, right after the younger children went to bed. Since this was not school, there were no grades or expectations other than that Sarah wanted to grow in her relationship with her Lord Jesus Christ. Sometimes their study caused them to be very serious and even grieved as they evaluated their lives in light of Scripture. Other times, they laughed and were silly.

As a discipling tool, we encourage you to consider doing individual Christian book studies with your children as they enter their teen years. You will be spending time together studying the application of God's Word in discipleship. Can you see how this would help keep your children's hearts?

Valuing Discipleship

Bible reading and church attendance are part of discipleship. We also consider our family altar time essential to discipling our children. We have discussed these in detail in Chapter Five.

Putting forth time and effort as a parent into the discipleship of your children will be worth it. Many strong Christians set aside time for discipling a new believer. Be sure your children have as high a priority and even higher than those outside your family. We don't want to risk losing our children's hearts because we were so busy discipling others that we neglected the discipleship of those we love the most.

We must be careful not to assume that discipleship happens automatically, but rather we want to purposefully plan it into our children's lives. May our children grow up being discipled for Christ by their parents. In the process, this will have a profound effect, we believe, on keeping our children's hearts.

Questions

1. Are you actively discipling your children?

   a. How are you doing that?

2. Are there ways you could enhance your discipling of your children?

3. Is Mom looking for way to disciple her daughters?

4. Is Dad looking for ways to disciple his sons?

◆ ◆ ◆ ◆ ◆ ◆ ◆

Decisions were prayed about and evaluated;
I didn't hear the world "sheltering" daily during
my growing-up years. Sheltering is more a descrip-
tor of how I was raised. Nathan

◆ ◆ ◆ ◆ ◆ ◆ ◆

Chapter 8

The Concept of Sheltering

Sheltering is a concept we want to shout as loudly and clearly as we can because this has been a vital key to keeping our children's hearts. It is perhaps the most unique difference in our parenting from that of other Christian parents we know. When evaluating whether to introduce something new to our children or our family, we ask ourselves, "What will this do to our child's heart? How will this affect him in relation to our biblical goals for him? What appetites will this develop?" Our answers to these questions have prompted us to make sheltering a way of life for our family.

A Definition of Sheltering

What exactly is sheltering? Are you thinking of it as we are? Here is our definition: *Sheltering is keeping our children away from negative influences while directing them toward positive ones.* That is rather simple and basic, yet sheltering appears to be one of the most difficult aspects of parenting.

We see sheltering even in nature. One summer Steve and our boys were building a new privacy fence in our backyard to replace the old one that was falling down. When they began taking boards off the pile of wood delivered from the lumber store, they had a surprise. A huge colony of carpenter ants had begun living in that wood. When the boys started moving lumber, the ants' "mega" nursery was exposed. Those ants immediately commenced moving their babies to safety. When faced with a negative influence, the ants hurried their young off to shelter.

When one considers sheltering in its global sense, one can soon see that everyone believes in sheltering. The only question is to what extent they endorse it. No parent in his right mind would leave a loaded handgun on the coffee table while children are playing in the room. No normal parent allows his toddler to walk along a busy street unattended. Truly, everyone believes in sheltering.

For the Christian parent, a good picture of the sheltering concept might be that sheltering is a natural progression toward holiness. "But as he which hath called you is holy, so be ye holy in all manner of conversation; Because it is written, Be ye holy; for I am holy" (1 Peter 1:15-16). The Lord wants holiness in the lives of His children. As parents, sheltering is one of the major vehicles we can use to help our children along the path of holiness.

Give Me Your Heart

We have already looked at Proverbs 23:26 that says, "My son, give me thine heart, and let thine eyes observe my ways." Now let's evaluate the two verses following to see exactly how the giving of the son's heart will benefit him. "For a whore *is* a deep ditch; and a strange woman *is* a narrow pit. She also lieth in wait as *for* a prey, and increaseth the transgressors among men" (Proverbs 23:27-28). We observe that giving his heart to his father is going to shelter this son from the immoral woman. It will protect him from sexual immorality. Obviously, this isn't a young child who is being sheltered, but one of an age and freedom to fall snare to the prostitute.

There are many misconceptions that are brought up when sheltering is discussed. In order to have a clear view of what sheltering is and isn't, let's look at some points for each.

Sheltering is much like a sheepfold. It will be an environment of safety and protection, where the wolves are kept out. The sheltering will be accomplished in a spirit of love and gentleness with the goal of winning and keeping the child's heart in the process.

Sheltering is not solitary confinement. We want this point to be clearly understood. Instead, activities, work, and ministry will take place with the family and, therefore, the parent's protection. Sheltering is not "Don't!" with harshness or anger trying to force and demand a child's heart. Sheltering provides rich, positive experiences of education, serving, and fellowship consistent with the parents' biblical goals for the children.

A Personal Story

While we will give many more examples in the next chapters about what sheltering is and what it isn't, perhaps a personal story from our lives would be helpful as we begin to learn more about sheltering.

The UPS man stops by our house every afternoon. Once, when there was a substitute for a couple of days, the children asked where the regular driver was.

"You mean Caveman?" the substitute asked. The children's eyes got real big as they realized that the UPS drivers had nicknamed our driver "Caveman." That became our children's name for him as well until we had a discussion one day.

We talked with the children about whether "Caveman" was a respectful name for our UPS driver, even if they didn't actually call him that when they talked to him. They agreed it wasn't, and determined to find out his real name.

Not many days after that, they came to Teri and delightfully announced, "His name is Mr. Smith. His name is Mr. Smith."

"Whose name is Mr. Smith?" came from Teri's confused mind, which had already forgotten the previous day's discussion.

"The UPS man!"

Can you imagine what Mr. Smith thinks when he is greeted by five lively children each afternoon shouting, "Hello, Mr. Smith! Hi, Mr. Smith. How are you, Mr. Smith?" Remember, Mr. Smith's coworkers call him Caveman.

Eleven-year-old John gave Mr. Smith a gospel tract. A couple of days later John asked Mr. Smith if he had read the tract. "Oh, yeah!" he replied. "It was good. I even showed it to the other guys at the terminal when I got back."

"Would you read another one?" John asked. "Sure," answered Mr. Smith. Since then, as a result of the children befriending Mr. Smith, Steve has had the benefit of witnessing to him. Time will tell what the Lord may do in Mr. Smith's life.

This example, we believe, will show you that a sheltering lifestyle doesn't preclude our children from sharing Jesus with others. However, they are doing it in an environment where their own hearts are being as carefully guarded as possible.

Sheltering versus Isolationism

Often when sheltering is discussed, some have a picture of an isolationist lifestyle. We are not advocating that at all. Instead, we are suggesting working, serving, studying, and ministering as a family. For us, this means we are around our children constantly, serving the Lord Jesus with them and protecting them at the same time. There are so many ways the Lord has given us to minister, serve, fellowship, and evangelize as a family through the years.

We are not isolating our children. As a matter of fact, our children are well known in our neighborhood and community because we purpose to interact as a family with those we come in contact with on a regular basis. For example, we just received a thank-you note from a neighbor several blocks up our street whom Steve, Christopher, and John had helped with a flat tire. Here is part of the note: "We've long admired your large and beautiful family. Your children are polite and friendly, virtues not encountered so often nowadays." We are showing our children how to be "in the world" (John 17:11) but "not of the world" (John 17:14).

We are able to shelter our children and also minister with them to the lost world. Sometimes it sounds like well-meaning brothers and sisters in Christ are really recommending that to minister we have to be of the world, participating in worldly activities. We have discovered this not to be true.

A Deceitful Heart

Scripture tells us, "The heart *is* deceitful above all *things,* and desperately wicked: who can know it?" (Jeremiah 17:9). So we are aware that sheltering our children will not keep them from being sinful. However, we also know that external temptations to sin may reinforce the sin originating in the heart to a point beyond the child's current level of self-control, resulting in sinful thoughts or actions.

"You must not think it a strange and unusual thing, that little hearts can be so full of sin. It is the only portion which our father Adam left us; it is that fallen nature with which we come into the world; it is that inheritance which belongs to us all. Let it rather make you more diligent in using every means which seem most likely, by God's blessing, to counteract the mischief. Let it make you more and more careful, so far as in you lies, to keep your children out of the way of temptation." (J. C. Ryle)

Sheltering Based on Love for Christ

We hope that by giving you, in later chapters, concrete personal examples of sheltering our children, we will help you to see specific applications of Scripture to everyday choices concerning keeping the hearts of our children. These are not legalistic rules but personal, prayed-over application of Scripture. We plan to address many of the areas of sheltering we have chosen for our family to give you a picture of how these decisions are made and then worked out practically in a family's life.

Of course, we can't hope to touch on the myriad of influences that are in our world today and concerning which your family may be making decisions. Each family will need to use Scripture to evaluate the possible influences in their children's lives. Then they should decide if this is an influence to shelter from or to encourage toward.

We can't emphasize enough that these decisions are based on our love for Jesus Christ and our desire to serve Him. We look at Scripture as we consider the influences we want for our children or ones that we think should be avoided. We don't only look at the consequences for today, but also the potential ones that could follow in a year or in ten years. This perspective is closely tied to the goals the Lord has put on our hearts for our children. The question before the Lord is, "If I sow this today in my child's life, what will he reap in the years to come?"

Sheltering Presented to the Children

These sheltering decisions, once made, are presented in a loving manner to our children at the appropriate time. Sometimes no explanation is needed because the children know of no other possibilities or direction. Other times we explain to them the biblical basis for these choices that they can obviously see are different from those of other families. We are gentle and compassionate as we discuss these issues with them. Since we want to help our children love other believers who are not like us, we talk about God's ongoing work in each Christian's life.

In the process of sheltering the children from negative influences, we don't leave them in a vacuum without anything they are allowed to do. Instead, we seek ways to replace negative influences with godly, positive ones. We pray for and watch the Lord provide wholesome activities that will encourage the children in godliness rather than pulling their hearts toward worldliness.

Empty lives cannot produce godly children (Matthew 12:43-45). We substitute carefully chosen books for television. Childish, innocent toys replace evil, wicked ones. Family ministry takes the place of expensive entertainment while work projects fill up extra time. For each potential influence that could pull our children's hearts away, the Lord can give a positive one that will draw their hearts to Jesus Christ and to their families.

May we never underestimate the power of God's grace, but may we never presume upon it, either. It may be tempting for parents to say, "This path of sheltering looks too difficult to me. I don't like saying 'No' to my children. I did lots of things that weren't good for me, and I turned out okay." To presume God will automatically counteract our wrong decisions would be very difficult to justify with Scripture.

The Connection Between Hearts and Sheltering

Have you understood the important connection between keeping your children's hearts and sheltering? If not, let us take it a step further for those who may still have some questions. When the boys disturbed the ant colony nursery, the ants didn't wait to see if harm was going to come to the eggs. They began to take action immediately once the protection of the nursery was upset. The boys' presence posed risk, and the ants immediately began to move the eggs to a more secure place.

In the same way, we would rather not wait to see if something or someone is able to steal away our children's hearts, "A prudent man foreseeth the evil, and hideth himself: but the simple pass on, and are punished" (Proverbs 22:3). It is our desire to be prudent by looking down the road, seeing evil or danger, and sheltering our children from it. We are determined to be proactive and to do everything we can to prevent it from occurring.

It seems like many families have assumed they can trust their teenage children because they have their hearts and because the children are thought to be spiritually mature. Often these families are disappointed because they end up losing their children's hearts. If it is rather common to hear about a pastor falling into sin of some sort, how can we assume our children will fare better? Sheltering is the critical balancing aspect needed.

Having our children's hearts does not mean we can't lose them. In fact, pity the poor parent who assumes he has arrived and can coast since he has succeeded in having his child's heart. Life is ever changing, and new influences may surface at any time. Children are not good judges of character. The parent who is not constantly on guard may well lose the child's heart. Any negative influence can rob you of your child's heart. Even a positive influence, when it becomes consuming, can do the same thing.

Obviously, not every family that assumes their child is spiritually strong enough to resist temptation loses that child to the world. However, from the number of letters we receive, there are many youth, raised in conservative, Christian, homeschooling families who are being lost. Are you a gambler? What sorts of odds are acceptable to you when your children are at stake? For us, we don't gamble, and we don't want to presume. We desire to be obedient to our Lord as He directs us in raising our children.

Choosing to Shelter

Sheltering is often misunderstood and is therefore seen in a bad light. Everyone shelters their children to some extent. How much you shelter will depend on the goals you have for your children and how you think your children will best reach those goals.

Sheltering does not mean solitary confinement or isolationism. Instead, the sheltering we practice is focused on work and ministry as a family among those in our community. We are with our children, though, so that they are protected and the negative influences are guarded against. We have seen many families lose their children to worldly influences simply because they didn't shelter.

To shelter your children, you will want to eliminate influences that draw your child's heart away from you and, in the process, away from the Lord. Instead, you want to encourage influences that draw his heart to his father and his mother, who can help him focus on Jesus Christ.

Questions

1. Are you sheltering your children?

2. How are you sheltering them?

3. Is your sheltering of your children consistent with your God-given goals for them?

4. How do your children spend their time?

5. What influences do these activities have?

   a. Are they negative or positive?

6. What appetites are being developed by your children's activities?

   a. Are they positive appetites or negative ones?

◆　◆　◆　◆　◆　◆　◆

The decisions in our home were always based on a desire to follow and obey the Lord – not on a list of rules. Christopher

◆　◆　◆　◆　◆　◆　◆

Chapter 9

The Biblical Basis of Sheltering

As we raise our children with an eye on keeping their hearts, we have discovered the importance of sheltering in this process. Sheltering produces positive results in the keeping of our children's hearts, since negative influences, which draw their hearts away, are eliminated. Let's look at Scripture references that relate to sheltering

God the Father's Example

There is no one better in the Bible to look to as an example than the Father of all fathers, the Shepherd of the shepherds, God the Father Himself. We need to learn from Him in all areas of our lives, including sheltering. We will use God the Father as our ultimate example of parental sheltering. As we look at how our Heavenly Father shelters His children, we get a clearer picture of how we as parents can shelter our children.

God the Father has already been used as an example in our biblical study of keeping a child's heart. Once again, let's look to Him as an ideal standard instructing us in the sheltering of our children.

Recalling our definition of sheltering, we remember that sheltering is to curb negative influences while encouraging ones that will draw hearts to Jesus Christ. "Take heed to thyself that thou be not snared by following them, after that they be destroyed from before thee; and that thou enquire not after their gods, saying, How did these nations serve their gods? even so will I do likewise" (Deuteronomy 12:30). Here we see God sheltering His children from the negative influence that learning about other gods could have on them. Not only does He not want them to be snared by those gods, He doesn't even want them to inquire about them.

Why didn't God want His children inquiring after other gods? He knew that there was a distinct possibility that what they learned about those gods could draw their hearts away. His goal for His children was that they love Him, and Him only, with all their hearts, souls, minds, and strength. God wasn't willing to let negative influences into the lives of His children that might draw them from Him.

"When the LORD thy God shall bring thee into the land whither thou goest to possess it, and hath cast out many nations before thee, the Hittites, and the Girgashites, and the Amorites, and the Canaanites, and the Perizzites, and the Hivites, and the Jebusites, seven nations greater and mightier than thou; And when the LORD thy God shall deliver them before thee; thou shalt smite them, *and* utterly destroy them; thou shalt make no covenant with them, nor shew mercy unto them: Neither shalt thou make marriages with them; thy daughter thou shalt not give unto his son, nor his daughter shalt thou take unto thy son. For they will turn away thy son from following me, that they may serve other gods: so will the anger of the LORD be kindled against you, and destroy thee suddenly" (Deuteronomy 7:1-4). Once again, we observe God sheltering His children from negative influences.

In these verses, God is specific about why He is sheltering His children. He tells them that the negative influences of the other nations will draw their hearts away from Him. God is using sheltering to keep the hearts of His people for Himself. This is the kind of sheltering we can choose to do as Christian parents. We will eliminate negative influences that have the potential to turn our children's hearts from the Lord.

Toward the Positive

Did God shelter His children by directing them to positive influences? We believe that Deuteronomy 6:5-9 is this kind of Fatherly pattern and instruction. "And thou shalt love the LORD thy God with all thine heart, and with all thy soul, and with all thy might. And these words, which I command thee this day, shall be in thine heart: And thou shalt teach them diligently unto thy children, and shalt talk of them when thou sittest in thine house, and when thou walkest by the way, and when thou liest down, and when thou risest up. And thou shalt bind them for a sign upon thine hand, and they shall be as frontlets between thine eyes.

And thou shalt write them upon the posts of thy house, and on thy gates."

In these verses, we notice that God wants His people to love Him with all their hearts, souls, and might. He tells fathers to teach this to their children. He is sheltering His children by focusing them on Himself – telling them to love Him.

These verses also give to us a vision of a parent who is with his children almost all the time, something we are encouraging in the sheltering process. Certainly God is with His children continually to an extent that isn't possible in our human parenting. In Deuteronomy 6:5-9, we have a parent who is with his children when they get up, when they are at home, when they go out, and when they go to bed at night – constantly. God is commanding this parent to be teaching his children about Him in the midst of all these circumstances.

Sheltering to the Ninth Power

"He that dwelleth in the secret place of the most High shall abide under the shadow of the Almighty. I will say of the Lord, *He is* my refuge and my fortress: my God; in him will I trust. Surely he shall deliver thee from the snare of the fowler, *and* from the noisome pestilence. He shall cover thee with his feathers, and under his wings shalt thou trust: his truth *shall be thy* shield and buckler" (Psalm 91:1-4).

Secret place is a hiding place from danger.

Abide refers to lodging or resting.

Shadow means to be in the shade of or defended by. A tree can provide shade or be a defense against the heat of the sun.

Refuge is a shelter to keep one safe from danger.

Fortress refers to a high fort or inaccessible place.

Deliver means to rescue or defend against danger.

Snare is something set to trap, imprison, or destroy by someone with the intent to do harm.

Noisome pestilence is the great calamity, wickedness, or disaster that might sweep one away.

Cover is to fence, hedge about, or protect.

His truth shall be thy shield and buckler because the Word of God will protect from dangers.

What do you think these verses mean when they mention such things as being a refuge, fortress, cover, and a secret place? Certainly, they can mean physical protections, but it seems obvious they extend far beyond simply the physical. This protection will include shelter from evil and negative influences.

When God wants to emphasize something, the Holy Spirit will prompt the writer to say it two, three, or even more times. Look at how, through repetition in these verses, the Lord is shown to be a shelter for those who trust in Him. Within this one section, we read, "secret place," "abide," "shadow," "refuge," "fortress," "deliverer," "cover," "shield," and "buckler." Nine words all carrying similar meaning – almost like sheltering to the ninth power! What an incredible picture these verses presents of God's sheltering of His children.

Let's look at another intriguing aspect of God's sheltering. His sheltering enables us to take our refuge in Him. He isn't sheltering simply to protect us. He is sheltering so we will want to flee to Him. We know that being within the safety of God's sheltering is the very best place to be.

The Israelites knew what it was to be attacked by the enemy. They wanted a God Who was a fortress to run to for protection. The word "city" in the Old Testament meant a place kept by watching, and normally it was walled about. To the Jew, it was a safe place, a refuge, yes, even a shelter. This is the analogy God is making to Himself in Psalm 91.

The Lord doesn't shelter us just so we will be kept from negative influences; He shelters us so that we will choose to abide in Him. If we accept His sheltering, we will not be taken captive by others. In a similar way, by sheltering our children and keeping their hearts, we want them to learn to choose that sheltering. We would like to see them flee to our shelter in time of need, because they have experienced first-hand its loving benefits in their lives.

We could never shelter our children from every bad influence – particularly considering our own hearts are full of evil. "For out of the heart proceed evil thoughts, murders, adulteries, fornications, thefts, false witness, blasphemies" (Matthew 15:19). Therefore, even in the shelter of our homes, our children will certainly experience the struggle with sin; however, through our discipleship, they will learn how to respond to that struggle. They will be tempted and learn self-control. All of this will happen within the relative safety of the home. Without this kind of sheltering, the negative influences our children are exposed to can stimulate and encourage the evil inherent in their hearts.

It is a joy when a child comes to a parent to discuss struggles he is having, looking for our help. Isn't that what the Lord wants us to do as well? We are to flee to Him and His Word for direction and strength. This is what sheltering our children is all about – teaching them to choose our protection and leading their hearts to the Lord.

Who could number the young men who, rather than being protected through sheltering, have been introduced to pornography by their own father bringing the material into the home, only to be discovered by the son? What other forms of stumbling have been introduced to the young minds that we are called to raise in the nurture and admonition of the Lord (Ephesians 6:4)?

What should happen in sheltering homes is that the children know the value of the haven their parents have provided and embrace it as being for their best. We shelter our children so they will be drawn to the Lord Jesus Christ and not be pulled away to other influences that are "heart stealers." How comforting for our children to value Dad and Mom as their refuge from worldliness!

The Hen's Example

To bring a clearer picture of sheltering to our minds, the Psalmist paints a picture of a bird, such as a hen, protecting her young as they hide under her wings (Psalm 91:4). We asked some who were familiar with hens and chicks to give us firsthand observations of how they interact. Following are snippets of what we were told. Consider as you read them the analogies to sheltering our children.

We have a mama sitting on a clutch of eggs right now. One baby has hatched and stays buried in her feathers. The chick will make tentative steps out but any sound and he dives back under. Later, when the mama takes the chicks out, they will stay very close to her. The babies are sensitive to things overhead (hawks, I would imagine), and any shadow that passes causes a rush under her wings. Yes, she does literally spread her wings and protect the little ones.

If the rooster picks up the danger, he gives an alert sound, and the hens hear it, so that there is a cacophony of calls until the danger passes. Just as a matter of course, the hen clucks constantly in a low voice, and when she speeds up her clucks, the babies come at once. She sees dangers that they are unaware of, and they know her voice and respond immediately. If they don't respond, she runs after them and brings them all together under her wing. She is quite dogged in her attempts to protect! When under the hen's wings, the chicks are quiet and still, knowing they are protected.

The parent is to shelter his young just as a hen does her chicks. Chicks are helpless to fend off an enemy's attack. The child cannot recognize danger and has no means to fight. When those chicks are under the hen's wings, they can't see a thing. Similarly, we can trust in the encompassing protection of our Father's sheltering wings. The same should be true of our children as we accept our role in sheltering them.

Jesus said, "O Jerusalem, Jerusalem, *thou* that killest the prophets, and stonest them which are sent unto thee, how often would I have gathered thy children together, even as a hen gathereth her chickens under *her* wings, and ye would not" (Matthew 23:37).

If we don't have our children's hearts, sheltering them will be difficult. Jesus used the mother hen to teach us how He desired to gather the Jews together. He wanted to draw them to Him and protect them, but they would not gather! Without our children's hearts, they will likely react to our sheltering and view it as restrictive rather than beneficial.

Sheltering helps to keep our children's hearts by keeping those hearts from negative influences that draw them away. However, if we have begun to lose the heart or have lost it for some reason, we may find a child resisting our sheltering. Then we will need to endeavor to win his heart back so that he will choose the sheltering rather than being unhappy about it.

A Good Example and a Bad Example

In Genesis 19, we see Sodom and Gomorrah is about to be destroyed. Lot is living among a people with a depraved and wicked lifestyle. Even though "righteous" Lot was vexed by their conduct, he had not protected his family from evil influences by moving away. He appears to be more concerned about his easy life than the virtue of his family. Lot was unwilling to shelter his family; he lost them as a result.

Now let's contrast Lot with Abraham. In Genesis 12:1, Abraham received God's call to leave his extended family and go to a land that God would show him. There would have been security and comfort in staying where he was. However, Abraham was willing to follow God's direction for his life into a land of uncertainty.

What is God's calling for your family? If that calling is different from the mainstream, are you willing to obey? Read what the Lord said about Abraham in Genesis 18:19. "For I know him, that he will command his children and his household after him, and they shall keep the way of the Lord, to do justice and judgment; that the Lord may bring upon Abraham that which he hath spoken of him." Can He say that about us?

The Sheep's Preparation

A biblical pattern for sheltering can be seen by what Jesus told His disciples in Matthew 10:16, "Behold, I send you forth as sheep in the midst of wolves: be ye therefore wise as serpents, and harmless as doves."

The Greek word for harmless is "akeraios." *Vine's Expository Dictionary of Old and New Testament Words* defines this word as "literally unmixed, with absence of foreign mixture, pure." It is used metaphorically in the New Testament to describe what is guileless, sincere, harmless, with the simplicity of a single eye, discerning what is evil, and choosing only what glorifies God. The Merriam-Webster dictionary defines "guileless" as being innocent and naive.

Romans 16:19: "For your obedience is come abroad unto all *men*. I am glad therefore on your behalf: but yet I would have you wise unto that which is good, and simple concerning evil." The word "simple" is "akeraios." Paul is saying he desires that believers would be pure and without any knowledge of evil. Doesn't that sound like the sheltering we have been describing?

In the final place in the Bible where "akeraios" is used, it is translated as "harmless." Philippians 2:15 says, "That ye may be blameless and harmless, the sons of God, without rebuke, in the midst of a crooked and perverse nation, among whom ye shine as lights in the world." Again, Paul is saying we are to be pure and naive regarding evil as we live in a crooked and perverse nation. We are to be in the world, but not of it. We shine by being pure lights, not polluted with the things of this world.

The only way to raise children that fit this description is by sheltering them from negative influences so that their hearts can be fully turned to Jesus Christ. Through sheltering, we can give them a desire for being and staying pure in their youth so they will choose to live that way as adults.

Main Purpose of Sheltering

As Christian parents our main goal in keeping the hearts of our children is so that we can direct and influence them toward loving God with all that they are. In Scripture, we read of God the Father sheltering Israel, His children, from negative influences that could rob their hearts from

Him as long as they chose to abide in Him. In a similar way, we can shelter our children from those outside influences that might steal their hearts away from their parents and from the Lord.

When we shelter, we will see our children learning the benefits and value of that sheltering. This then makes sheltering something the children choose to flee to in times of need and temptation. This aspect of sheltering emphasizes the importance of having our children's hearts. Without their hearts, they may outwardly conform to sheltering, but inwardly feel bitter about it.

Scripture clearly tells us that we are to be innocent regarding what is evil. This is our directive to be sheltering parents. In our role of bringing our children up in the nurture and admonition of the Lord (Ephesians 6:4), we should heed our responsibility to keep those children innocent of evil. "Prove all things; hold fast that which is good. Abstain from all appearance of evil" (1 Thessalonians 5:21-22). Without sheltering, the children will be exposed to countless detrimental influences, any one of which may pull their hearts from the Lord.

When the Maxwell men and boys go to the Mission to witness, they have not needed to experience the same ungodly walk of the men to whom they are witnessing. Our boys have been sheltered, but they have no fear of sharing Christ with men who have led worldly lives.

Sheltered youth should be raised according to these three verses. Matthew 10:16: "Behold, I send you forth as sheep in the midst of wolves: be ye therefore wise as serpents, and harmless as doves." Romans 16:19: "For your obedience is come abroad unto all *men*. I am glad therefore on your behalf: but yet I would have you wise unto that which is good, and simple concerning evil." Philippians 2:15: "That ye may be blameless and harmless, the sons of God, without rebuke, in the midst of a crooked and perverse nation, among whom ye shine as lights in the world."

Observing the Scriptural examples and directives to sheltering, we can see that sheltering will be beneficial for our children. Rather than setting our children in the world to sink or swim, we can shelter them in an environment that will draw their hearts to their Lord Jesus Christ and prepare them for a life of service.

Questions

1. Read through Psalms and list other verses such as Psalm 91:1-4 that demonstrate how the Lord shelters His children.

2. Can you find other places where Jesus sheltered His disciples?

3. Based on the Scriptures shared in this chapter, are there changes that need to take place in your sheltering of your children?

♦ ♦ ♦ ♦ ♦ ♦ ♦

Another very important aspect that stands out in my mind is the sincerity with which my parents have lived out those decisions in their lives. I can't think of a single time they have requested more of me than they have of themselves. Christopher

♦ ♦ ♦ ♦ ♦ ♦ ♦

Chapter 10

Our Example and Instruction As Parents

Sheltering begins by parental example. We can't expect to shelter our children and have them willingly receive it if we don't choose to shelter our own lives. We are to be in the world but not of it (John 17:11-16). We have to live in the world and around sin, but we are not to be pulled into the world's sin. The poor person who feels he is stronger than sin is a likely victim.

The types of sinful temptations will vary. We cannot cover every one, but we think by using one as an illustration for this chapter, you will get the general idea. For the sake of example, let's use the lust of the flesh as the basis for discussion.

The Bomb Squad

Have you seen photos of bomb squad members who were handling explosives in the attempt to disarm or move them to another location? We imagine the protective gear and shields they use to protect themselves make Goliath's armor look like a loincloth. If you think about it, aren't the bomb squads being overly cautious? When was the last time you heard about a bomb squad having a suspicious item blow up and injure some of them? So why does the bomb squad take all of those precautions? Could it be that they are aware of the serious danger they are in, and they are protecting themselves in the event that something were to go wrong? Their cautions do not indicate lack of confidence in themselves or their procedures. Rather, they know that you can't be too careful, and that, if something bad happens, the consequences can be disastrous.

Every man or woman who desires to remain morally pure should have the same attitude of caution that a bomb squad has. In many ways, this is a form of sheltering ourselves. The key to acquiring that attitude is understanding what Jesus said in Matthew 15:19, "For out of the heart proceed evil thoughts, murders, adulteries, fornications, thefts, false witness, blasphemies." In the Greek, the phrase "For out of the heart" refers to where these sins originate. Until we lose this body of flesh, we have to come to grips with the fact that we are our own worst enemy. We have to realize what we are capable of because it is bound up in our flesh. We have to understand that it isn't our great wisdom or our lofty spirituality that keeps us out of trouble. It didn't work for Solomon or David or countless other mighty men who have failed through the ages, and it won't work for our children or us.

David

David saw that "the woman *was* very beautiful to look upon" (2 Samuel 11:2), and David lusted after her beauty. Oh, what danger "we" are in when it is readily accepted among Christians to "appreciate" the beauty of other women. Had David earlier placed safeguards toward sheltering in his life, he might have avoided much pain and heartache. In addition, he could have had a more powerful positive influence on his son in this particular area.

If David had realized the trouble he was in right then and taken action, the sin, the separation, and the consequences would not have happened. For Jesus said, ". . . That whosoever looketh on a woman to lust after her hath committed adultery with her already in his heart" (Matthew 5:28). David, the author of most of Psalms, was not spiritually above temptation or failure. So it would appear that just because a man loves the Lord with all his heart and has a heart after God's, that isn't enough to keep him from lust, adultery, and murder.

Have you ever heard of a pastor or man in spiritual leadership running away with a young woman and leaving a wife of many years behind? Most everyone has. Could it be that the pastor wasn't aware of the consequences for such actions? Not likely. Most men in any form of ministry have observed others' consequences from moral failure. Doesn't this pastor know better? Of course, but once the lust of the flesh kicks in, all reason goes out the door. Likely, this man tolerated an "acceptable" level of lust in his life, thinking he could control it without consequences. In addition, since he felt he was not susceptible to sexual temptations, he probably had chosen not to shelter his own life.

Solomon

"But king Solomon loved many strange women, together with the daughter of Pharaoh, women of the Moabites, Ammonites, Edomites, Zidonians, *and* Hittites; Of the nations *concerning* which the LORD said unto the children of Israel, Ye shall not go in to them, neither shall they come in unto you: *for* surely they will turn away your heart after their gods: Solomon clave unto these in love. And he had seven hundred wives, princesses, and three hundred concubines: and his wives turned away his heart. For it came to pass, when Solomon was old, *that* his wives turned away his heart after other gods: and his heart was not perfect with the LORD his God, as *was* the heart of David his father. For Solomon went after Ashtoreth the goddess of the Zidonians, and after Milcom the abomination of the Ammonites" (1 Kings 11:1-5).

What about Solomon? He was the wisest man in the world and was given that wisdom by God. Solomon was a man who heard God speak to him. Of all people, Solomon knew better and should have been faithful to His God, yet he failed miserably as he grew older. His life showed the power of godly wisdom and the cruelty of worldly living. He didn't structure his life to practice what he preached. Solomon loved many strange women in spite of God telling him not to "go in to them, neither shall they come in unto you; *for* surely they will turn away your heart after their gods."

David, because of his sin with Bathsheba, had set a poor example for his son, Solomon. Could this have been instrumental in Solomon's failure as he disobeyed God when he sought wives of different nationalities? Did David's bad example play a part in Solomon's struggle with lust?

Our example as parents will have similar results in our children's lives – positive or negative. Do we shelter ourselves when it comes to negative influences that will pull our hearts away from our Lord and our families? If so, we are setting a good example for our children.

A Wise Father Shelters

A father will likely not take steps to shelter himself if he doesn't understand what is in his heart and how easily he can fall. We believe anyone who thinks he is above falling doesn't understand his own heart.

Another reason a man won't flee sin is because it is pleasurable. Might he be trifling with sin with the hope that it isn't hurting anyone? Regardless of the reason, may we parents consider our example to our children. The level of sin that we will accept in our lives has great bearing, by example, on what will be acceptable to our children.

We don't watch television because we want to shelter ourselves from those things that could lead us into sin. With the programming and commercials that are broadcast these days, television can easily stir up sinful lusts. That is also why we don't go to movies, many summertime activities, and even the circus any more. They are designed to entertain, but one of the ways they do that is to stir up lust in the men who are watching.

Our children must be taught the depravity of their hearts and not to trifle with sin. However, what example is set by their father? Do they have a father who walks as close to the line of sin as possible, or a dad who desires to walk as close to the Lord Jesus as possible? What are we teaching our children by word and example?

If the children see Dad condoning, by his viewing entertainment, the things of the world, we should not be surprised to see them trying to embrace the real thing when they finally have a chance. If they don't understand the mighty fire that the flesh contains, will they want to protect themselves?

We were pleased that when Nathan married, he and his wife chose not to have a television. Would he have made that decision if we, as parents, had watched television in our home while sheltering our children from it? As parents, we must constantly be aware of the effect our example will have on our children.

Educational Process

It is our biblical responsibility to teach our children what sin is: that sin is an offense against God, that He hates sin, that we are drawn to it, that we must flee it, and that we should repent if we fail. If a goal for our children is holiness, then we will teach them the truth about sin in generalities that they can understand. We have to be honest with our children so that they understand sin is enticing, fun, and pleasurable. Obviously, if this weren't the case, no one would be drawn to sin. We will also want to teach our children the consequences of sin from a biblical perspective. It should cause them to view sin not only with a disdain but also with an awareness of its pull. This type of educational process helps our children become "wise as serpents" while remaining "harmless as doves" (Matthew 10:16).

We have seen this kind of teaching be powerful in our own children's lives. The boys, who go with Steve to City Union Mission, have seen the results of drug and alcohol abuse first hand. They talk about it regularly after mission visits, both in the car and in family discussions at home. Whenever we read Proverbs 23:29-35 on what alcohol does to a person, we discuss alcohol. We don't try to pretend people don't like to drink. However, we discuss the results of the decision to drink alcohol. Our children have contempt for drug and alcohol usage.

Rather than looking at teens who are drinking and being envious of them, our children's hearts feel sorry for them. They have seen the end of the path these teens are walking along and know it is not a happy ending. Growing up with regular age-appropriate discussions about sin has helped us keep our children's hearts. Their hearts are not being pulled to enticing forbidden fruits. We haven't had to ban some of these activities, although we would. Instead, our children have had no interest in the sinful, immoral things many teens are doing.

Consider the lust-of-the-flesh example we have dealt with heavily in this chapter. How are you teaching your children, both boys and girls, to flee youthful lusts? Are you purposely dealing with it or simply disregarding it? We don't teach fleeing by ignoring it or pretending our children won't have youthful lusts. Rather, we face it head-on, and teach them how to place protection and shelters in their lives to help them flee those youthful lusts. They need to see these same shelters in place in Dad and Mom's lives.

What Is the Result?

"Instruction, and advice, and commands will profit little, unless they are backed up by the pattern of your own life. Your children will never believe you are in earnest, and really wish them to obey you, so long as your actions contradict your counsel." (J. C. Ryle)

We want to raise our children in homes where Christ is alive and Deuteronomy 6:6-7 is lived out. They must see that they cannot have confidence in their spiritual maturity or wisdom to keep them from being drawn in by the world. The world "knows" how to stir up a person's desires and then what to feed those desires. Our children should understand that they are capable of being drawn into sin. "But every man is tempted, when he is drawn away of his own lust, and enticed" (James 1:14).

How about you? Teaching and example are powerful mentors. Are you teaching your children about the consequences of sin? Have you let them know that sin is pleasurable and enticing? If most of life as a Christian is focused on fun, what's to stop children from wanting even more serious fun? The Lord Jesus sees your heart and knows what goes on there. Are you setting the example for your children in fleeing youthful lusts and other sins? Are you playing with fire? Have you accepted that which is unacceptable to your Lord? If so, will you be able to offer counsel to your children in helping them to avoid being ensnared by the world? Will you succeed in keeping their hearts?

Questions

1. How are you age-appropriately teaching your children about sin?

2. In what areas of your personal life are you setting the positive example for your children by sheltering?

3. In what areas of your personal life are you setting the negative example for your children by not sheltering?

4. Are there areas in which you feel convicted to make changes regarding your example?

   a. If so, what are they?

◆　◆　◆　◆　◆　◆　◆

If I had been fed a steady diet of worthless enter-
tainments while I was in my teen years, I doubt I
would have enjoyed working in my business or
developing vocational skills. Christopher

◆　◆　◆　◆　◆　◆　◆

Chapter 11

Sheltering from the Negative Influences of Things

We encourage Christian parents to evaluate every influence that is coming into their children's lives. How does it impact your biblical goals for your children? What appetites might it grow? Where will it take their hearts? Hold each influence up to the light of Scripture, being careful not simply to go with the flow of what others are doing and accepting.

There are so many things in our world today that are offered into the life of a child. We plan to go through several about which we have made decisions. Our thoughts about doing this are that you might see the process the Lord took us through on each one. We are not telling families the choices they should make, but rather, we are encouraging them to consider well every aspect of their children's lives. Hopefully, in working through the things we have chosen to shelter our children from, you will be stimulated to prayerfully evaluate these influences in your child's life and perhaps find even more as well.

Television

"I will set no wicked thing before mine eyes . . ." (Psalms 101:3). Television is filled with wickedness and evil. Even if there are shows that would be okay, the commercials won't be acceptable. How can we expect to keep our sons' hearts if they are continually exposed to immorality and immodestly dressed women on television? Will our daughters want to be morally pure when continually exposed to the romance that is idolized on television? Won't our children's hearts be drawn to being entertained if they are allowed to spend their time in front of the television? Will we grow an appetite in our children for laziness by letting them watch? Consider well the spiritual outcomes of children watching television.

Soon after being saved, we chose to get rid of our television. However, when we had three young children and they all came down with chicken pox at the same time, we decided to purchase a TV to help Teri occupy them during their illness. We carefully screened the shows the children were allowed to watch. What we couldn't screen were the commercials. In the middle of a show, there would be a commercial for a horror movie to be aired later in the evening. While watching another program, the children would be exposed to a beer or cigarette commercial.

Our next step was to videotape the shows that we felt were acceptable for the children to watch. That way we could fast-forward through the commercials while enjoying the benefit of what we now see is a mindless occupation for the children.

It wasn't long before the Lord began to open our eyes to what the children were actually learning through the portrayal of the characters in the television shows. We were allowing the children to watch family-based programs that were reruns from shows that were popular when we were children. However, generally the father was depicted as a bumbler, while the mother came off looking like the family leader. This was creating unbiblical role models for our children.

We were also concerned about exposing our children to the high level of folly depicted in television shows such as sitcoms and cartoons. "Folly *is* joy to *him that* is destitute of wisdom: but a man of understanding walketh uprightly" (Proverbs 15:21). Obviously, folly comes naturally to children (Proverbs 22:15). We were trying to help our children gain "understanding," so we did not care to fuel their bent toward folly.

There were more problems we were facing in our hopeless quest to match TV watching with our Christian walk and goals for our children. Violence and poor attitudes seemed prevalent, even in the tamest of programming. One of our biblical goals for the children was that they love others. Therefore, time spent watching these TV shows was undermining our direction for our children.

What about those beautiful, captivating, educational programs? Surely, they would be acceptable. However, we noticed they always seemed to be based on evolution and humanistic philosophies. These were not thoughts we wanted filling our children's minds. "Finally, brethren, whatsoever things are true, whatsoever things *are* honest, whatsoever things *are* just, whatsoever things *are* pure, whatsoever things *are* lovely, whatsoever things *are* of good report; if *there be* any virtue, and if *there be* any praise, think on these things" (Philippians 4:8).

With these revelations, we next moved to more careful screening of the television shows. The problem here was the amount of time this required and the difficulty in making decisions related to specific shows. In the end, we realized that TV was not beneficial for our family in any way. About 1988, we stopped watching television completely.

When we were still letting the children pass time watching TV, we were not aware of the appetite we could grow in them for wasting time by being entertained. One of our biblical goals for our children is that they would enjoy serving and working. "Not slothful in business; fervent in spirit; serving the Lord" (Romans 12:11). This is a reason why, even now, with the availability of filtered programming targeted to Christians, we remain TV-free.

We occasionally see glimpses of television while in a store, and we are appalled at what has become accepted by our culture. In our desire to keep our children's hearts, we see the need to shelter them from television and the negative influences that are innate in its programming.

Toys

Let us begin by sharing some of our goals for our children's playtime that in turn translates into goals for toys. As we began our parenting adventure, we did not realize that the toys our children played with had an influence on their character development, their future appetites, and where their hearts were turned.

If we allowed the children to have a toy with an evil face, they played with it as an evil individual, and their play took on an evil bent. If we gave our children an electronic or video game, they spent hours sitting and playing with it. They lost interest in any type of active or creative play. They didn't want to spend time with their siblings or parents. If the video game was violent, we could see that tendency coming out in the children's interactions. Our goals, even for how our children spend their playtime, are important.

We choose to shield our children from as much worldliness as possible. 1 John 2:15 tells us to "Love not the world, neither the things *that are* in the world. If any man love the world, the love of the Father is not in him." Therefore, we desire that our children be involved in pure, wholesome types of play. For example, we give the girls baby dolls rather than Barbie dolls. We would like for our daughters to desire to be nurturing mommies rather than possibly giving them a hunger for dating relationships.

We want the children to develop skills while they are playing. That means we will invest in puzzles, wholesome games, quality reading books, and even tools. Creativity is on our list of goals for playtime. Therefore, we avoid electronic toys with lots of "bells and whistles" – the kind with a never-ending thirst for batteries. In addition, we choose to avoid toys that are faddish. We didn't have to decide if some of the Star Wars toys were okay or not. They fit into the category of faddish and therefore weren't even considered.

It is amazing to us, even with sheltering our children from many, many of the toys available, that we still have a house full of toys. If you choose to keep your children from toys that may create wrong appetites and that don't lend themselves to your family's goals, your children won't lack for toys. There are still toys available that are good and wholesome.

We desire for the children to be developing hearts toward the Lord, their parents, their siblings, and service even while they are playing. This, then, needs to be taken into consideration when we are picking out toys. Will this toy help my child toward the goal or hinder him? What appetites will it potentially develop?

Reading Materials

Reading materials are a very important area in which we have chosen to shelter our children. Our desire is that they grow up to be men and women who love Jesus Christ, want to pursue holiness, and are faithful servants of God. As we read books to our children, we became aware of the importance of the quality of our children's reading material. We realized that these books had an influence on our children's lives and hearts.

We have taken Philippians 4:8 as our gauge of what we want to read ourselves and have our children read. It says, "Finally, brethren, whatsoever things are true, whatsoever things *are* honest, whatsoever things *are* just, whatsoever things *are* pure, whatsoever things *are* lovely, whatsoever things *are* of good report; if *there be* any virtue, and if *there be* any praise, think on these things."

First, we found that, although some of the books were interesting to the children, there was no value in them, no virtue. They were simply entertaining. Other books actually portrayed negative behaviors and attitudes. They were not "just" or "pure." For example, one book we read talked about a person wanting to punch someone else in the nose. Our little boys laughed and laughed, and it came up in conversation between them after that. They had never before heard of punching in the nose. We didn't want them learning wrong behavior, thoughts, or attitudes from what they read. There are many books in which brothers and sisters have bad attitudes and say awful things to and about each other. Others model dislike, disrespect, or disobedience toward parents. Is any of this what we want to foster in our children? Of course not!

We started reading a book from a very popular children's series. Before we had gone halfway through the first book, it had brought up Jack Frost, Santa Claus, and the need for birthday spanks if a child is to grow. None of that is true. It may have been what actually happened in the family of this story, but it became very confusing to our children as Teri tried to explain why the book character believed in these things, and we didn't. We gently told the children we had to stop reading this book and why. We were sorry we had not stopped earlier.

Along this line, but down a slightly different path, is the choice of books for our daughters to read. Christian romance novels are very popular, but do they promote what we want our daughters to think about? What appetites do they whet in our daughters' hearts? Is romance where we want their hearts focused during their years before marriage? Is this the goal?

It is hard enough for a young woman who is committed to waiting on God for a spouse not to think about young men. When she is constantly immersed in romance, it becomes even harder. Christian romance novels set our daughters up with false expectations that are seldom lived out in reality. We have found it much better to encourage our daughters to read Christian biographies. These challenge the girls in their Christian walk and give true insights into the realities of love and marriage.

"For your obedience is come abroad unto all *men*. I am glad therefore on your behalf: but yet I would have you wise unto that which is good, and simple concerning evil" (Romans 16:19). "Take heed to thyself that thou be not snared by following them, after that they be destroyed from before thee; and that thou inquire not after their gods, saying, How did these nations serve their gods? even so will I do likewise" (Deuteronomy 12:30).

Because of Scriptural admonitions such as are found in these two verses, we have chosen not to allow our children to read mythology. We don't want our children learning about foreign gods. We would rather not have those thoughts going through their heads. We do not mind the children knowing that the Greeks, Romans, and other ancient cultures worshiped many gods. However, we do not want them to know details of this worship. We prefer that they not even know the names of the gods until they are exposed to them as adults.

The time we spend reading out loud with our children is valuable for us just because we are together. However, we want to redeem every moment of the day. We don't want to waste any of our time or our children's time by reading books that don't meet the test of Philippians 4:8. We don't want them to read things that may draw their hearts away. Reading time can be wonderful Inspiration and encourage ment in the Lord to our children. This is especially true as we find books about great Christians or stories that bring out character and right attitudes. We can have the benefits educators tell us come from reading. In addition, the children are inspired to godly behavior by what is read without the negative influences that come if we do not carefully screen reading material.

Will sheltering our children by protecting them from certain books and limiting what they are allowed to read mean they never have anything to read? On the contrary, we have shelves and shelves full of the most delightful children's books. Many are spiritually encouraging. Others are simply wholesome with no negative innuendos or influences.

Sheltering children in their reading material is more time-consuming than simply allowing them to read whatever they choose. It involves pre-reading or at least skimming through books before giving them to the children. We sometimes look at ten potential books before we find one that meets our reading criteria. However, when that one book is found, it is a real treasure. Because reading is important to us and is enjoyed by our children, we invest the needed time in the hunt for quality reading material. We even encouraged Sarah to write a children's reading book that would meet our reading standards (see page 278).

What about you? Have you put a high value on what your children are reading or what you are reading to them? Have you thought through the criteria that reading material should have in your home? It takes effort and sometimes means we miss out on what everyone else may say is great. We think choosing to please God in this way will have significant benefits in the lives of our children now and throughout the years. It is a part of sheltering to keep their hearts.

Is It Worth It?

Each of us is easily swayed by the influences around us, children even more than adults. When we see how quickly sin can overtake mature, godly adults, should it surprise us that children's hearts can be pulled to the world by what they watch on TV, play with for toys, or read in books? What is it worth to us to shelter our children from these negative influences and replace them with influences that tug their hearts toward godliness, obedience, and parents? Are we willing to make the needed investment, knowing others may criticize and perhaps condemn us for our choices?

For us, it has been, and is, worth it. We have watched with joy as our adult children moved through the teen years without rebellion. It has been a delight to us to fellowship with our children in their adult years, not having had to watch them go through the agony of any moral failures. Our hearts rejoice as we have observed, through first-hand experience, the turning of the father's heart to his children and the children's heart to their father. We believe sheltering our children from particular "things" has been a big part of this. We want that same joy for every Christian family!

Questions

1. Do you allow your children to watch television?

2. Is TV watching consistent with your biblical goals for your children?

3. If your children watch TV, what appetites do you think are being developed?

4. If you choose for your children not to watch TV, when questioned by a well-meaning family member concerning this decision, what would you tell them?

5. Have you evaluated your children's toys in light of your biblical goals? If not, we suggest you do so.

6. Do you shelter your children in their reading materials?

7. What are your criteria for selecting reading material?

♦ ♦ ♦ ♦ ♦ ♦ ♦

Some parents are afraid that if they tell their children "no," they will grow up with bad childhood memories. That certainly wasn't the case with me.
Nathan

♦ ♦ ♦ ♦ ♦ ♦

Chapter 12

Sheltering from Negative Influences of People

Scripture is overwhelmingly full of directives to us as Christians in general to live holy lives. "But as he which hath called you is holy, so be ye holy in all manner of conversation; Because it is written, Be ye holy; for I am holy" (1 Peter 1:15-16). Sheltering our children's hearts is all about leading them toward holiness. It is our greatest desire to live lives pleasing to Jesus Christ and to help our children do the same.

Matthew 18:6-7 says, "But whoso shall offend one of these little ones which believe in me, it were better for him that a millstone were hanged about his neck, and *that* he were drowned in the depth of the sea. Woe unto the world because of offences! for it must needs be that offences come; but woe to that man by whom the offence cometh!" For us, living holy lives and not offending our little ones has included sheltering them from as many negative influences as we possibly can. At the same time, we are building into the children God's Word, His ways, and a deep love for Him.

Committed to Homeschooling

The most basic decision we made in sheltering our children was to homeschool them. We see no possibility of sending our children to school without exposing them to a myriad of negative influences that would draw their hearts from the Lord and from their parents. We cannot imagine having them under others' teaching and with peers for eight hours a day and still hope to keep their hearts.

Proverbs 13:20 tells us, "He that walketh with wise *men* shall be wise: but a companion of fools shall be destroyed." To us this verse says that we, as parents, are responsible to the Lord in helping our children walk with wise men. If we allow them through their childhood and teen years to be companions of fools, then we could be enabling their destruction. We also read, "Foolishness *is* bound in the heart of a child . . ." (Proverbs 22:15). Most children are full of foolishness. If our children spend every weekday during the school year with foolish children, they will not be walking with the wise, and we will be endorsing the loss of their hearts in the process.

Homeschooling protected our children in many ways. They kept their childish innocence throughout their childhood years. Sheltered in the homeschool environment, they didn't have to face vulgar, profane, ungodly, jeering, mocking, or hateful words and actions from other children. This type of harmful treatment would not have furthered our biblical goals for our children.

We frequently hear from others whose teenage children want to date because of other children's influence. There was no peer pressure in our children's lives for them to develop an interest in the opposite gender before God's time. Kept from being around others who were dating in high school and perhaps earlier, they maintained their moral purity. They chose not to give their hearts away to anyone except the one the Lord shows them is to be their spouse.

We know some believe their children should be in the public school system to be salt and light there. However, the result is often the loss of a child's heart to the world rather than the bringing of souls to the Lord. We are strong proponents of evangelism and teach that to our children. However, we have discovered there are ways to do this that don't involve the risk inherent in the public schools of losing our children's hearts to the world. We don't believe that the Lord has asked us to sacrifice our children in order to bring the Gospel to those in the public school system. He has many other ways He can lead an individual to salvation that won't involve losing our children's hearts.

Other parents send their children away to school because they feel the job of homeschooling is too difficult for the mom. Yet, as we talk to homeschool moms, we hear that most of them feel inadequate for the task even as they remain committed to it. However, keeping their children's hearts is so important to them that they are willing to ignore their inadequacies and let the Lord be strong in their behalf. "And he said unto me, My grace is sufficient for thee: for my strength is made perfect in weakness. Most gladly therefore will I rather glory in my infirmities, that the power of Christ may rest upon me. Therefore I take pleasure in infirmities, in reproaches, in necessities, in persecutions, in distresses for Christ's sake: for when I am weak, then am I strong" (2 Corinthians 12:9-10).

We know parents whose reason for sending a child to school is for the educational benefit of their child. They think that their children won't be able to get ahead in life without graduating from an institutionalized school. They have neglected to consider two important facts. First, statistics show that homeschooled students are excelling academically above their school peers. Second, the teen who becomes involved in drinking, drugs, premarital sex, or illegal activities will likely find this to greatly affect his future in a negative way.

However, be cautious. Many have chosen homeschooling as their only form of sheltering their children. When these parents have allowed their children to participate in activities that bring the same influences the children would have encountered in a school environment, the results are the same. Most of the families we refer to in this book who have lost the hearts of their children are homeschooling families. They have not chosen to shelter their children beyond homeschooling.

Consider the benefits we gain by sheltering our children from the negative influences of an outside school environment. Not only are they kept from these strong pulls to the world, but also they are with us during those school hours, so we are more able to interact with them throughout the day as portrayed in Deuteronomy 6:6-7.

Dangers of Sports

Nathan and Christopher were great baseball players. They loved to play about as much as we loved to watch them. The season began in late February and ended mid-summer when the All-Stars series was over. Unfortunately, we realized that those things that were needful and excellent in developing men of God, according to our biblical goals, were pushed out due to practices and games. We were trading time in God's Word as a family for ungodly peer influences and the boys being under the authority of coaches. For us it became clear that organized sports were opposed to us achieving our goals in raising our children.

We would encourage each family to evaluate your goals and pray long and hard before allowing your children to participate in sports. Even if you were able to keep your child from all the negative peer pressure, do you desire to give them the appetite for something that will consume hours and hours of their time as an adult? Most adults don't play on a team, but they do spend considerable amounts of time watching it on television. Why foster an appetite that will have no eternal benefit?

There is another danger in sports that can cause you to lose your child's heart – the coach. It is a fact that those under a coach's authority are highly influenced by him. In other words, the hearts of the team members are drawn to their coach. Even if the coach is a positive role model, if your child's heart is pulled to him, it is being drawn away from you. When that happens, your ability to guide your child's life is potentially diminished. Why allow this?

We encourage you to seriously evaluate your goals against Scripture and see if sports are the best use of a child's time. Perhaps there are far better ways to achieve the goals God has given you for your children.

For those who would like a more in-depth discussion on sports, Steve has a recorded workshop titled "Sports – Friend or Foe?" (see page 280). The feedback on that audio recording has been excellent, and the majority of those surveyed after hearing it say they never considered some of the information that was presented.

Friendships

If children come to our home to play with our children, we employ rules that enable us to protect their hearts. Years ago, we learned the necessity of this when our older children were elementary-school age.

There was a nice Christian family who lived near us. Their children were the same ages as ours, and we let them play together. It was only after they stopped playing together that we learned some of the things that went on at the other family's house when our children were there. There was nothing immoral, but there was much that was not consistent with our goals for our children. Our children were simply not strong enough to say no when the other children wanted to play what we would not have allowed. Since then, we have shouldered this responsibility and protected our children from situations like that.

Another time one of our children went to play at our (then) pastor's house. Who would be concerned about that? We later learned that the pastor's child told our child things that were highly inappropriate for a child to know at that age and certainly not acceptable for children to be discussing. While the pastor apologized for the incident, it really wasn't his fault. It was ours for letting our child go there unsupervised.

Experiences like this are why our children don't go over to other children's houses without us. We have made this a blanket family rule. Then we don't have to discern whether one family or child is a positive influence while another might be a negative one.

When there are other children at our house, we try to be in the same room with all of them. If for some reason we can't, we make sure that there are always at least two Maxwell children, preferably including an older Maxwell child, together with the other child or children. Just as Jesus sent His disciples out two by two (Luke 10), we make sure there are at least two of our children together for accountability's sake. These rules have benefited our children greatly.

Because of the influences that would come to our children from outside friends when we allowed these relationships with our older children, we began sheltering them from most children who would have been potential friends. With homeschooling, family activities, ministry, and work projects, there wasn't much time available to spend with friends anyway. During what time there was, we preferred that our children play with each other. We knew that sibling relationships last for a lifetime, and we wanted to nurture those relationships. In addition, from our older children's playing with neighborhood friends, we had discovered that the more they played with others, the more their hearts were turned away from their own brothers and sisters.

It is likely that, even as you shelter your children, you will find a family that is very similar to yours. The temptation then arises to let go of the sheltering rules. We suggest that you be cautious in this. Just because another family is like-minded doesn't mean their goals for their children are the same as your goals for your children. If the goals are similar, you still aren't assured that the other family is actually making decisions consistent with those goals. They may be allowing appetites to grow in their children that would oppose your goals and could be an influence on your children if they spent time together unsupervised.

For our family, we have come to realize that friends aren't a necessary or beneficial part of raising children. Sheltering our children from outside friendships helped us keep their hearts and build strong sibling relationships. We have also come to see the value of sheltering our children by overseeing their playtimes and friendships. This is an inconvenient and time-consuming task but worth it for our children's hearts and innocence. No matter how much we want our "independence" in times of fellowship, sheltering, for the season it is needed, is important.

Protection from Predators

Sheltering helps protect our children from predators. We warn the children, in very general terms, about those who would prey on them. In addition, we also do all we can to protect them. "Wolves" are drawn to the innocence of godly children and can be deceitful. Our sheltering in this area takes the form of us parents being with our children whenever we are around others who are not immediate family members. If this isn't possible, then we make sure there are several of our children together, never one alone.

One really can't tell who a person is from casual interactions – and sometimes not even from close friendships. Aren't we often shocked when we hear of a moral failure of someone we considered a fine, upstanding Christian? May we be ever vigilant as we watch over those in our care.

Immodesty of Swimming

As our walk with the Lord Jesus matured through the years after our salvation, modesty began to be an issue for us. Steve desired purity of heart continually, while Teri wanted to dress in such a way as not to wrongly attract attention to herself. This manifested itself in our daily clothing choices, but it also became something to contend with in the swimming arena.

As our boys approached the teen years, we wondered how we could take them to a public swimming area, where the dress was at the level of underwear at best, and expect them to have pure thoughts. To be honest, except for our enjoyment of swimming, we didn't wrestle with this decision long. There was only one choice we felt we could make. No more public swimming. It is amazing the freedom that comes once a decision like this is made. No more feelings of compromise. No more agonizing over whether we should or shouldn't. The decision is made; the direction is set.

There are times, especially when we are on the road staying at motels, when it would be fun for our family to go swimming. But we would not want to go back on the choice to protect the hearts of our sons and the innocence of our daughters by deciding to swim. The cost would be too great.

If your family is involved in swimming, think about the appetites you are allowing to be fueled in them through the swimming environment and influence. What goal does it promote? If you want exercise for your child, is there not a better way to achieve this goal that will also allow you to shelter him?

Pitfalls of Teen Jobs

In the process of raising responsible, diligent children, we parents often see the benefits of our teenage children having a job. We would like you to consider this, though, in the light of sheltering and keeping hearts.

At a job, your son or daughter will be exposed to any and all influences that a boss or coworkers bring to the work environment. We have heard several horribly sad stories of wonderful, godly, homeschooled children who were led astray at their job.

A successful, influential, Christian business owner told Steve about some of the unsavory types of individuals who work for him. Almost in the same breath, he told of how he tries to hire homeschooled teens because they are good workers. Steve wondered if the parents knew they were putting their innocent children at risk due to these workplace associations. Another parent told us that his son married a divorcee with children, which concerned the parents greatly. How did the two of them meet? They were working together.

Sheltering your children during their teen years doesn't mean they can't earn money. Instead, it means that, as a family, you will look carefully at the influences of any job. One of the best options is to help your children develop home businesses so that they can remain in the sheltered environment of your home or with the accountability of sibling coworkers. For example, siblings could work together in a business such as lawn maintenance, window washing, or home repair, where they will have the accountability of each other. Steve's book *Preparing Sons to Provide for a Single-Income Family* (see page 274) gives much more detail on this subject.

Remember, when considering a job for a teen, that you may have kept his heart all this time only to lose it when the work influences come into his life. Be very, very cautious if you let your child work outside your home, even if the boss is a Christian. From what we have observed, even though a Christian owns the company, it may be far from a "Christian" business and environment.

Extended Family

We are thankful that we have had only a few minor extended-family issues with which to deal. However, we can see that some comments might be helpful for those who are faced with negative influences from extended-family members.

Perhaps the sheltering that is the most difficult and takes the most courage involves relatives. No one wants to purposefully alienate a father, mother, father-in-law, mother-in-law, sister, or brother. Despite these desires, we believe our first responsibility, before the Lord, is to bring our children up in the nurture and admonition of the Lord (Ephesians 6:4). This means we will continue to work toward keeping our children's hearts and sheltering them even when extended family is involved. It may cause those family members to be displeased with us. However, it would be our hope to maintain family relationships while sheltering our children. If this weren't possible, we would choose our children's hearts first. Then we would strive to continue the relationships on an adult-only level without the children present.

If this were an issue for us, we would first set limitations and boundaries on our time and interactions with family members who pose particularly negative influences. We would be honest, with gentleness and love, about our concerns and reasons for these limitations and boundaries. While family members may not like our decisions, most will agree we are responsible for making decisions regarding the best interests of our children.

By choosing to limit time spent with those who would present negative influences on our children, we would be sheltering them. That means we wouldn't spend every holiday with extended family, and when we were together, we wouldn't stay long. We would keep our children near us so that they wouldn't be off with others, being exposed to things from which we shelter them. If this became awkward, we might consider planning activities, which we would oversee, for all of the children at the gathering. That way we would have a reason to be with the children.

We would plan to invite relatives, one family at a time, into our home where we have control over the influences. Often our desire in these relationships is to share the love of Jesus Christ and to have witnessing opportunities. This happens best in a smaller group setting when we have them in our own home by themselves.

If you are faced with this situation, we encourage you to ask the Lord to try your heart. The Psalmist said, "Examine me, O LORD, and prove me; try my reins and my heart" (Psalms 26:2). We have found that it is very easy to deceive ourselves about our motives for not wanting to associate with those who aren't like us. There are some whom we might not enjoy being around simply because they are different from us. However, the Lord may desire to use us in some way in these people's lives. Even though we are uncomfortable around them, it doesn't mean we aren't to interact with them. Steve and the older boys are somewhat out of their element as they visit with the mission men of a "different world." Often, they have nothing in common with homeless men off the street. However, Steve and his boys desire to show these men the love of Christ by listening to them and sharing Jesus with them. Just because we aren't comfortable or don't like a family member's lifestyle, that doesn't mean we can't be around them. However, when our children are involved in get-togethers with family members, the influences they will be exposed to must be considered and our response carefully evaluated.

In making decisions, it has been our experience that the Lord has never asked us to do anything that would be harmful to our children. We can be used by the Lord to minister to extended family and still protect our children from negative influences. While it is never easy to have family members unhappy with us because of our choices to shelter our children, we are the ones answerable to the Lord for those children. These verses may be an encouragement to you if you find your family displeased with you because of your stand for your children's hearts. "Suppose ye that I am come to give peace on earth? I tell you, Nay; but rather division: For from henceforth there shall be five in one house divided, three against two, and two against three. The father shall be divided against the son, and the son against the father; the mother against the daughter, and the daughter against the mother; the mother in law against her daughter in law, and the daughter in law against her mother in law" (Luke 12:51-53). While this is not the first choice in family relationships, if we must decide between family division or compromise, we choose family division.

College

For our family, we have not sensed the Lord's direction for our oldest children to go to college. We have observed that when a person attends college, he is shaped by the worldviews of the professors, textbooks, and students. If a child goes to college, he will be forever changed. The time away from home will cause his heart to begin the distancing process from the parent's influence. This has been obvious to us from those we know personally and from e-mails we receive.

The motive for any higher education attendance should be based upon clear direction from the Lord. This direction would be consistent with the goals God has given a family for their children. Inconsistency between biblical goals and college is often, we believe, a main indication that it isn't God's leading. Whether the "higher" education is local or away, be more certain of this decision than any other decision you will ever make with your child. There is too much at stake to lose your child to the world so close to the end of your parental role.

What Does It Mean?

We don't want you to have the picture that everything is a "don't." On the contrary, what we discovered through this sheltering process is that the "don'ts" opened our hearts and home to many delightful "do's" that we would have missed. Leaving behind these negative influences has only been good and positive for us. There isn't one of them that we would like to pick back up. In addition, as we observe our adult children's lives, we see that they are making the same choices in avoiding the influences that pull hearts from a focus on the Lord and instead are moving toward those that direct them to holiness.

Admittedly, these decisions are difficult. It is never easy to be different, and different we are. Family and friends may likely not understand your direction for your family and children. There will be seasons when you feel very much alone. May we encourage you that there are others – maybe more than we think – who are making these same choices? Sometimes we see our position as being like Elijah's when he complained that he was the only one who hadn't forsaken God's covenant. God assured him that there were 7,000 who also hadn't bowed the knee to Baal (1 Kings 19:9-18). If you begin doing what is needed to keep your children's hearts, who knows what influence that will have, not only on your own children but on other families who are watching you. It all starts somewhere. Why not with keeping your children's hearts through sheltering?

Questions

1. Are you homeschooling your children?

   a. If not, why not?

   b. Are those reasons consistent with your biblical goals for your children?

2. Who are your children's companions?

   a. Are they wise or foolish?

3. Are your children involved in sports?

   a. If so, what are your goals for them being in sports?

   b. Are those goals consistent with your biblical goals for your children?

   c. Are there any better ways to achieve those goals for your children?

4. Is having friends for your children consistent with your biblical goals for them?

   a. If your children have friends, are you sheltering them during their playtimes?

5. What kinds of influences are other children bringing into your children's lives?

6. Are you sheltering your children from possible predators?

7. Do you let your children swim in public places?

   a. If so, is that consistent with your biblical goals for your children?

8. Have you considered influences in a young person's workplace?

   a. Are they positive or negative?

   b. Do they line up with your biblical goals for your children?

♦   ♦   ♦   ♦   ♦   ♦   ♦

As I look back over my childhood years, I have several regrets. The first vivid one was a bad experience at a sleepover. Sarah

♦   ♦   ♦   ♦   ♦   ♦   ♦

Chapter 13

Sheltering from Other Negative Influences

"I am a homeschooling, single mother of three children. I have two girls ages 14 and 12, and a 10-year-old son. The question that I have is about sending my children to a Christian camp. The church that I attend has a camp that is about a 45-minute drive from my house. I don't know the camp director and his family, but some people from my church do. They have only said good things about him. Also, some of the workers and counselors at the camp will be people from my church.

"My middle child is the one who really wants to go to camp, but I do not feel comfortable with it even though some of the campers and staff will be from our church. I do not like the mixing of boys and girls even though they are separated into different dorms. This year they are allowing high schoolers to mix with kids her age in junior high. Also, in the past they have allowed Christian rock or contemporary Christian music. I am trying to raise my kids with hymns of the faith and other songs that are devoid of the rock beat.

"I'm not sure what to do. Should I send her and my other children to camp and let them learn to be with other Christians (even from our own church) who have different standards and convictions? I just don't know if they will learn how to be with others and still keep their own convictions, or be influenced negatively. I don't even allow my girls to be in the youth group for many reasons, but the one that I shared with my pastor's wife is that I don't want my girls to be spending their time being and doing dumb, silly things.

"My pastor's wife told me not to judge, especially the outward appearance, because she knows where some of those kids are coming from and that we need to be patient with each other in our growth in the Lord. Also, we are not to push our own standards and convictions on others, but to be in prayer for each other and let God reveal to them as they grow.

"I understand what she is meaning, but I disagree with her. I don't understand why I'm feeling pressured to allow my kids into camp and youth group. Could you please help me? Do they need to be involved and interact with the other kids in such settings in a fairly 'safe' environment, or am I wrong to keep them home?" Concerned mom

What Kinds of Influences?

We really admire this mom's heart to raise her children for the Lord. What a challenge that is for any parent, but even more so for a single mom. We would encourage "Concerned Mom" to stand firm in her convictions and decisions. She can be very gentle and loving in explaining to her daughter, and to others, why she won't be going to camp. This mom's compassion for her daughter's disappointment, and sweetly conveying her love to her in the discussion, will be key in keeping her heart through this time.

Evaluating whether to send her children to camp is not being judgmental. We are to make right judgments. Jesus said, "Judge not according to the appearance, but judge righteous judgment" (John 7:24). We are to observe and learn from others. "I went by the field of the slothful, and by the vineyard of the man void of understanding; And, lo, it was all grown over with thorns, *and* nettles had covered the face thereof, and the stone wall thereof was broken down. Then I saw, *and* considered *it* well: I looked upon *it, and* received instruction" (Proverbs 24:30-32). This mother is doing exactly what the Lord would have her to do. She is using careful discernment as she raises her children in the nurture and admonition of the Lord (Ephesians 6:4). She is evaluating whether this activity is consistent with the goals God has given her for her children and what she will reap in the life of her daughter.

God has entrusted us, the parents, with the responsibility of our children's spiritual training and well-being. The choices "Concerned Mom" is making along those lines that she mentioned in her note are exactly what we are doing with our children. We are doing this because we believe Scripture teaches it. We have seen in real life that what we are exposed to influences our hearts – even things that are commonly accepted as being all right for Christian children.

For example, it is very difficult for a young person to be around Christian rock music and not be drawn to it. It is hard for them to be with others who are dating without wanting to date. On the other hand, when kept in a sheltered environment, without those influences, the children's hearts are more easily drawn to the Lord, to their parents, and to godly thoughts and pursuits.

The pressure that this mom was feeling is known by another name – peer pressure. That is exactly what she would be exposing her daughter to if her daughter went to camp. Her daughter would not have the years of maturity that this mom has. Yet, even with those years of maturity in the Lord, this mom was still feeling incredible pressure to agree to something that was against her God-given goals. Why is it, then, that parents feel their children will be "light" and not influenced by their peers? Children are not prepared to withstand the influences to which they will be subjected. We are not willing to expose our children to these kinds of influences. Are you?

Age-Segregated, Peer-Oriented Groups and Activities

Much to our amazement, as we raised our children, we discovered that they did not need to be involved in age-segregated, peer-oriented groups. In our early parenting, our children were involved in Sunday School, church children's programs, and other Christian children's activities. We saw these groups as positive alternatives to worldly children's functions.

However, it wasn't long before we realized that the first part of each week was spent dealing with behavioral issues that our children picked up during Sunday School. After seeking the Lord, we chose to take them out of Sunday School. It was very difficult for us, because we were now doing something that wasn't the norm. After making this change, many misconduct difficulties at home during the week were now avoided.

Still, there were other church-related children's activities in which we allowed the children to participate. When the children came home from these activities with words they had never heard at home and behavior difficulties, we began to rethink our reasons for letting our children be involved. As we prayed about our concerns, including seeing the children's hearts drawn to peers and teachers, we realized we could choose to keep the children from these activities. It seems funny to say it, but it was a real revelation to us. Just because there are other church children involved, maybe even homeschooled children, this did not mean that participating in the activity was consistent with our biblical goals for our children or beneficial for them.

"I do not like to see them coming to church by themselves, they often get into bad company by the way, and so learn more evil on the Lord's day than in all the rest of the week. Neither do I like to see what I call 'a young people's corner' in a church. They often catch habits of inattention and irreverence there, which it takes years to unlearn, if ever they are unlearned at all. What I like to see is a whole family sitting together, old and

young, side by side, - men, women, and children, serving God according to their households." (J. C. Ryle)

As we share these changes we made for our family, please keep in mind that Sunday School and children's church activities have a place for some families. Children who come from homes where the parents are not saved or where they receive no spiritual leadership can learn and grow spiritually in children's classes. As a matter of fact, historically that is what Sunday School was designed to do – bring biblical teaching to children with no access to church or the Scripture, with the goal of leading them to Christ and then to spiritual maturity.

For our family, because the children were receiving daily biblical teaching and discipleship, in addition to attending church services with us, they did not have the need for the extra children's classes offered at church. Those classes were actually undermining our goals of turning our children's hearts to Jesus by making their focus their peers in class and their teachers. We have been greatly blessed when we have found churches where the children's classes were optional, and where we have not been condemned as parents for choosing not to have our children in those classes but rather encouraged in our decisions.

Camps and Overnight Stays

As far as the Christian camp, we have chosen to shelter our children by not letting them spend the night at camps or even a friend's sleepover. There are untold numbers of stories of bad things that happened in a child's life when they were away from home at night. When we keep our children with us, we know that we have protected them from some of the horrible things with which others have had to deal.

For us, the ages of the children that are together at a Christian camp would be a problem, in addition to the mixing of children from conservative Christian homes and those from worldly homes. When we shelter our children from television by not having it in our home, we don't want them to learn what television teaches from other children with whom they are associating.

Steve went to Boy Scout and "Christian" camps as he was growing up. At the boys-only camp, the discussions would not have been deemed edifying for Christian young men. Then when he went to the "Christian" camp, all any of them cared about was the opposite sex. Everyone was always paired up when walking or at the campfires.

We don't want our children to develop an interest in dating because they heard the teens in their camp tent at night talking about dating. We know it wouldn't stop with a simple wish to date. It would move on to feeling resentment toward us, their parents, because we won't let them date. These are just a couple of examples of the influences our children could come under in a camp setting. Something as simple as the decision to let them go to a "great" Christian camp could be the first step toward losing our children's hearts.

Sheltering Through Courtship

Having experienced the dangers and pitfalls of teen dating, we knew from the time our children were very young that we would like for them to avoid this. When we began homeschooling, we started hearing of other families who were encouraging their children not to date. This kind of sheltering protects our children in many ways. It keeps each child's heart for the one the Lord intends to be his or her spouse. They are less likely to fail morally. Financially, when they don't date, they are much better off. There is more time for serving and working when the attention isn't riveted on the opposite sex.

We have discussed with our children the benefits of waiting for marriage until the Lord directs in the timing and person. How this process of courtship (for lack of a better word), engagement, and marriage is navigated can be greatly influenced by having our children's hearts. This may be the biggest decision, next to salvation, that they will make. Their ability to seek the Lord for His direction in this is imperative. Their success comes through the years of their parents having their hearts and teaching them to be dependent on Jesus Christ, looking to Him for guidance.

Marriage is the time when the child's heart, in an earthly sense, is transferred from his parents to his new spouse (Genesis 2:24). It is a natural progression that God ordained. However, it is important for parents to realize that they must willingly relinquish their child's heart at this time rather than trying to continue holding on to it. Their job of keeping the heart is over because that heart has been transferred.

Youth Groups

We shelter our children from youth groups. We believe they undermine our biblical goals for our children. Youth groups have great potential to steal the hearts of our children. Here are the reasons why we do not want them to participate.

Instead of this:	We want this:
We do not want our children's hearts turned to peers or youth group leaders rather than toward us.	We want them turned to us so we can effectively disciple them.
We do not want them drawn toward an "entertainment" mentality.	We want them to enjoy ministering and serving others with their family.
We do not want their hearts pulled toward dating.	We want them to find a mate in a Christ-honoring, pure way.
We do not want them exposed to influences we are protecting them from by homeschooling.	We want them to pursue holiness, without looking down on those who don't.
We do not want them to think they can't have a good time unless they are with friends their own age.	We want them to enjoy being with their parents, siblings, and others of all ages.

Please understand that we are not being judgmental of youth group leaders. We know there are many well-intentioned people expending great amounts of time and effort with the hope of winning teenagers to Christ. It is just that youth groups are not beneficial for our family, based on our goals for our children.

We have felt strongly that youth groups would undermine many of the reasons we homeschool. There is every likelihood a young person will come under the influence of peers in a youth group. This would be particularly true with a group that includes public- and private-school students. Children would be exposed to the worldly ideas and practices from which we want them to remain separate. Dating relationships are major interests of those attending youth groups. With our children committed to courtship, it would be counterproductive to subject them to other teens who constantly discuss boyfriends and girlfriends.

Based on what so many have told us, we have come to believe that most youth groups have an entertainment mentality. They are much more focused on having fun in the hope of bringing others into the group than they are on spiritual growth or serving. We have heard of eating ice-cream off the floor, immorality, lockdowns, pool parties, water fights where the girls participating become horribly immodest, and more.

Service projects or emphasis on spiritual growth may be thrown in here and there, but they don't really end up being the main thrust of the ministry as observed by where the time is spent. There are a few exceptions from what we hear, but they would not be sufficient justification for our family to reap the other consequences. Even if the youth group spent its time in Bible study, prayer, and serving, the boy/girl focus would still be too harmful for us to allow our teens to be exposed to it on a weekly basis. Further, even if the group segregated boys and girls, it would still draw the hearts of our teens to the leader.

We believe that a family's viewpoint about attending a church with or without a youth group ultimately depends upon the parent's goals for their children and their level of involvement in the spiritual lives of their children. We understand that a youth group has sometimes been instrumental for bringing a young person to Christ, usually a young person with little or no spiritual foundation at home. On the other hand, the youth group has also been the downfall of many a young person from a spiritually strong home. The young person couldn't withstand the influences faced within the youth group, nor did the parents realize the temptations that were there.

What About Not Participating?

One mom told us that she was troubled over the influences in their church youth group that her son was attending. It was having a very negative effect on him. She said that the church worked at bringing lost youth into the group. In addition to their influence, he was exposed to aggressive young girls, clothing that was indecent, worldly music, and childish conduct. When asked why she let him go to this youth group, she was speechless. She said it never entered her mind that she had the option of not allowing him to participate.

We have chosen not to go to churches with youth groups. We realized we would be asking too much of our children to be in a church with a youth group and then expect their hearts not to be pulled in that direction. We knew how hard it would be for our children to read about the youth activities and see the cliques from the youth group but not be a part of them. Our children have acknowledged to us, now that they are adults, that they agree. They think they would have struggled with feeling resentful for not being able to participate in the youth group if we had attended a church that had one.

They would have read and heard about the bowling and swimming parties, skiing outings, retreats, cookouts, and lockdowns. How could they not have been drawn to such fun? In addition, by not participating, they would always have been the "odd" ones, never fitting in when the other youth were talking and sharing. They would have seen the young people in dating situations and could have had their hearts drawn toward wanting that for themselves.

Could being in a church with a youth group while not allowing our teens to participate be good training for them by getting them used to being in the world and not of it? We don't think so. From what we have observed and heard from others, the children just end up being resentful of the parents. This bitterness leads to losing their hearts and then rebellion. We have not felt it was beneficial to put our children under that kind of pressure. It is difficult enough to be a peculiar people in the world, let alone in the church.

In a church with no youth group and no dating, our goals for our children are upheld. They see other young people making the same choices they are making and don't feel like they are the "only" ones. Sometimes we are asked how we will teach our children about courtship. We don't have to teach them. It is all they know. It is what they have grown up with and will continue to grow up with.

Having no youth group works out practically in our church because the youth are part of their family unit within the church. They sit with their families. They serve with their families. They learn how to worship with their families without having to be entertained.

Each family must evaluate its goals and decide whether youth group participation will further those goals. We can't present strongly enough the blessings a church with no youth group has been to our family.

Other Groups and Activities

As we evaluated other groups and activities in which our children could participate, the reasons they weren't in Sunday School, children's church, or youth groups generally applied. Even in the homeschool group we led for ten years, the children seldom participated in any of the activities, of which there were very few anyway. Because of our personal positive feelings toward family activities and ministry, we encouraged this same philosophy within our homeschool group. Therefore, we left the organization of children's classes and field trips to those who would be motivated to take on the projects but reminded them that family field trips and learning were the best way to go. This meant that the group's focus was on equipping the parents in their homeschooling calling rather than providing entertainment and outside activities for the children. Be cautious even about homeschool groups as they sometimes become quasi-youth groups.

No matter what the group or activity might be, we want to evaluate whether the children should be involved in it based on our goals for our children. Will the time spent move the children toward the biblical goals we have for them? If so, is this the most beneficial way to achieve the goal for the child? What kinds of influences will they be under – positive or negative ones? What appetites could be developed? What is our motive for considering the activity? Is this the best use of our child's time?

As we think about all the activities in which we chose not to have our children participate, we are happy with our decisions. We gained a much greater focus on family unity, Bible learning, ministry, and work skills because we weren't running the children to this club or that group several nights a week. As we have watched others whose children participated in outside-the-family activities and groups, we saw these children's hearts drawn to their friends, group leaders, and the worldliness they encountered in the meetings. These kinds of results were counter to our biblical goals for our children. We believe that sheltering our children from these outside activities has been a part of what has enabled us to keep our children's hearts.

Can We Make These Choices?

Sheltering our children is not judging others. God has entrusted our children to us, and we are responsible for them. When we shelter our children, we make decisions based on God's Word for them. It has nothing to do with condemning others. Most Christians in churches would agree not to drink alcohol. By their choice not to drink, they aren't judging those who do. Each will stand before the Judge and give a personal account.

Because of negative influences from other children in our children's lives beginning in their younger years, we began making our first decisions to highly shelter our children. This didn't mean they were isolated, but rather, protected. Our chicks were under the shelter of the hen's wings (Psalm 91:4). We were with them all the time.

We didn't want to raise the children in an environment that was monastic. We replaced age-segregated, peer-oriented activities and classes with other activities that would have a positive impact on our children's lives. These included staying home more, keeping up with our schoolwork, ministering as a family, developing vocational skills, and working together. We will discuss these in more depth in a later chapter.

Our three adult children have thanked us for these choices in raising them. They are well-adjusted, godly adults very capable of "making" it in the real world. There was a time when Nathan worked at the same company as Steve. It was common for Steve's coworkers to tell him how much they appreciated Nathan. At age eighteen while he was working on someone's computer, he was frequently asked what college he had graduated from because of his maturity level and technical skill. He was highly respected in his business environment.

As we look back on the various sheltering decisions we have made, we have not regretted any of them. We have seen only positive consequences in our children's lives and our lives as well. Leaving the activities in which we have previously been involved has forced us to find better ways to use our time – ways that will keep our children's hearts and be productive toward our goals. It has caused us to make changes in our parenting, but we are glad we did. Certainly it is easier for our younger children since there are fewer direction changes than there were for our older ones.

We want to challenge you to consider well this area of sheltering. Take it to Scripture. Then, if sheltering is biblical, make the decision to shelter. Determine what God wants for your children. Don't be put off by others' opinions or the ease of life when the children are entertained. Instead, make the choice you won't regret. ". . . Let every man be fully persuaded in his own mind" (Romans 14:5).

Questions

1. Are your children involved in activities your church offers for children?

   a. Are these activities consistent with your biblical goals for your children?

2. Are your children allowed to attend camps?

   a. Is this consistent with your biblical goals for your children?

3. Are your children allowed to participate in sleepovers?

   a. Is this consistent with your biblical goals for your children?

4. Are your children allowed to participate in a youth group?

   a. Is this consistent with your biblical goals for your children?

5. Is your own involvement at church too much, too little, or just right to support your goals for yourself and your children?

6. What groups and activities are your children participating in?

   a. Are they helping your children toward a biblical goal?

      i. If yes, is there any better way to achieve this goal?

   b. What kinds of influences are involved?

   c. What kinds of appetites are being grown?

   d. Is there any better use of the time being invested in this activity?

♦ ♦ ♦ ♦ ♦ ♦ ♦

I can't imagine where I'd be now if my parents had just let me do whatever I wanted. I wouldn't change their sheltering for anything in the world!
Sarah

♦ ♦ ♦ ♦ ♦ ♦ ♦

Chapter 14

The Reality of Our Sheltering Choices

As Christian parents struggle with the pain of losing the heart of a child and watching the suffering of a teen walking through rebellion or immorality, they often feel helpless. Much is said about the poor choices teens and young adults make that are likely to have serious repercussions, but are we as parents holding each other accountable for the decisions we are making?

Raising children is like participating in an enormous survey. We parents vote with the lives of our children with each decision we make concerning them. It is only years down the road when the results come in, and by then it may be too late. Usually talk is about children's choices, but little is said about what the parents have been doing. Who laid the foundation upon which these children will make their own decisions? What goals were in place and how were they implemented? What appetites did the parents sow or allow to be sowed in their children's lives that resulted in a sorrowful harvest?

We are not judging anyone for his or her decisions. That is not our place. However, it is our desire to encourage dads and moms to stop and question some of their parenting strategies before trouble arises. Because sheltering to keep our children's hearts is very difficult to discuss and define without specifics, we would like to evaluate some real-life situations. In looking at these families and their choices, we should be able to discern what influences were in those children's lives and which ones had the greater pull on the hearts of the children.

Family One

Family One moved to a new town and began attending a large, growing, evangelistic church. There was tremendous emphasis on reaching the lost and on missions. The family had some reservations about involving their children in the youth group because of the way they noticed the boys and girls interacting. However, both the pastor and youth pastor made it a point to try to persuade Dad and Mom that it was important for their children to participate. They were told they shouldn't judge others by not allowing their children to attend the youth group. The pastor said it was a great opportunity for their children to be a light to the unsaved teens who were attending and to other young people who were not as mature in their walk.

Dad and Mom struggled with this decision. They knew how difficult it would be for their children to be a part of the church but not be in the youth group. They finally were convinced they needed to trust their children to God and let them participate. After all, their children were teens and had been raised to know right from wrong. In addition, they had the hearts of their children and trusted them. Plus it would give them, as the parents, a good opportunity to be an example to many liberal couples.

This family soon began seeing their daughter's heart pulled toward the youth group crowd. She had had strong convictions in several areas, but the influence of her peers began to change those. This daughter started to be unhappy with her parents when she couldn't do things some of the other youth were allowed to do. It didn't take long for these parents to realize they had lost their daughter's heart. They now had a daughter struggling with rebellion, and they were faced with abandoning their goals or trying somehow to win their daughter's heart back.

These parents made a decision that went against what they really felt in their hearts was best for their children. They felt pressured by the pastors, other families in the church (adult peer pressure), and even by their own love for their children. They wanted their children to be accepted by the other young people in the church. Discussions concerning this situation will revolve around the daughter's wrong choices. Could it be, however, that the parents' decision to be a part of this church was a higher priority than keeping the hearts of their children?

Family Two

"We have homeschooled since kindergarten. Our oldest son is now 16. He is very musically talented. He had a summer internship with our music minister and has gone to Christian music camps. He used to love his Lord Jesus, but now the excitement is gone. He tells us he is 16, as if he can make all of his own decisions now.

"We have directed our children toward courtship since they were little, but recently our son has decided he wants to date. We have gone through all the reasons why he shouldn't date. We are very sad with this turn of events. Our hearts are broken over our son's rebellion. We desperately want his heart back." Hurting parents

We have noted the importance of avoiding dating relationships to keep our children's hearts and to help them toward moral purity at marriage. These parents started when their children were young to teach them about courtship and encourage them toward it. Those were great decisions.

However, they allowed their son to participate in Christian music camps. In previous chapters, we discussed two possible ramifications of this decision on keeping the son's heart. First, the camp setting and being away from home begins a separation process that draws a child's heart away from his parents. Next, the other teens at camp will most likely be involved in dating relationships. This then put a young man in an environment where his heart was being separated from his parents and drawn to the new influences. That would have been risky enough if there were young men only, but these were co-ed camps.

We believe it is simply too much to expect young people to be around others who date or in situations where they develop friendships with the opposite sex and then ask them not to date. Something as innocent as a music camp is going to put teen boys and girls together, allowing relationships that could lead to dating desires.

Many will say that if parents have trained their children well, it won't be a problem for them to be in situations like a Christian music camp. That sounds good in theory, but it seldom proves out. Children in their teens usually are not yet strong enough to resist the powerful influences by which they are surrounded.

We may feel we are being unkind to our children, or others may try to make us feel this way about sheltering them, but the opposite is true. We are, in reality, doing them a kindness. How many people do you know, or perhaps you yourself, who have regrets over things done during their youth years? How many live with "if only" regrets? Is it better, for example, to shelter a person from the things that cause cancer while you teach them how to avoid it, or to let them discover it for themselves? For us, we would rather shelter and teach, so our children can avoid the heartache.

It isn't that we keep our teens locked in the house, allowed to do nothing. On the contrary! We want them to be busy – very, very busy and productive – ministering with the family, studying, working, serving, and growing in their relationship with Christ. All this is done in the context of the family, homeschooling, or very carefully chosen activities (remember the problems with the seemingly innocent music camp) – perhaps where it is only one gender involved (for even then, boy-girl talk might be a prime discussion theme). Our goal is that our teens are so involved in serving the Lord with their lives and productive with their time that there is no thought for dating.

Family Three

"Our church has great children's programs. We wanted our children to attend these activities to meet some Christian friends. At one point, a boy became interested in our teen daughter, and she liked the attention. In hindsight, our first indication that we were losing our daughter's heart was that she didn't share with us what was happening.

"We had a Fourth of July party at our house, and our daughter wanted to invite some friends from church. During the party, we could tell our daughter and the boy were interested in each other. At first we were troubled about it, but as we discussed it we realized we didn't want to turn her against us. We felt we should give her some freedom and would allow them to see each other in our home. We let him visit her a number of times. Before long, we were aware that they were becoming closer and physical. We told them they couldn't be together any more even with supervision. Now we have a bitter, rebellious daughter. We have lost her heart." Troubled parents

In this family, we see an influence that most would consider acceptable, even positive – a church program for teaching children. However, in this case, it has cost a family the heart of their daughter. Rather than growing her in spiritual maturity and turning her heart to the wisdom of Scripture and her parents, this young woman was drawn to the appetites of the flesh. Her heart was pulled in exactly the opposite direction from the one her parents wanted for her.

The Difficult Choices and Path

Obviously, we can't eliminate all worldly influences from our children's lives. However, we have discovered that we, as parents, can make many choices to limit these influences. What will we do? Because others tell us that an activity or group is acceptable, perhaps even beneficial, do we allow our children to participate? Is this consistent with our biblical goals for our children? Will we look at each outside influence and determine whether it pulls our children's hearts closer to the Lord and to their family or in another direction?

Once the heart is lost, trying to get it back is much more difficult than preventing its loss in the first place. Steve would always rather do new construction than remodeling. With remodeling, there is demolition, cleanup, and then restoration. Unfortunately, the restoration can never be as good as new construction, since you have to work in an area that already has imperfections. Purpose to keep your children's hearts instead of having to win them back should you lose them.

Through the years, we have made decisions for our family that run counter to what most others are doing, mainly in the area of sheltering the children. As we have watched other families live through the heartbreak of their children's actions, we are strengthened in our resolve. Some of these families have been friends, and our hearts have bled with them as we watched the pain in their lives.

We are grateful to the Lord for His Word and encouragement to us, even when His Word shows us we should pull back from what most deem acceptable. We rejoice that, while the path we have walked often seemed lonely because few other families followed it, we were blessed not to have had to experience living through rebellion or moral failure in our children.

Questions

1. Do you know families struggling with their children?

    a. Can you discern the influences at work?

    b. From what you know now, how would you counsel these families?

2. Do you know families that are not struggling with their children?

    a. Can you discern the influences at work?

3. Imagine you are eighty-six years old and lying in a nursing home bed. Based on your current parenting, what kind of life do you envision your children having lived?

    a. Are there any changes you might want to make in your parenting based on this evaluation?

◆ ◆ ◆ ◆ ◆ ◆ ◆

Dad and Mom have given me purpose and direction in these young-adult years of my life. I enjoy working in our family ministry and helping at home, and I just finished writing a children's reading book. Sarah

◆ ◆ ◆ ◆ ◆ ◆ ◆

Chapter 15

Encouraging Children Toward Purpose in Life

If we see the biblical directive and importance of sheltering our children from negative and harmful influences, this would mean we keep them away from those influences. Many would then wonder what there is left to do. How will your children learn to interact in the real world?

We have already mentioned this area as we looked at other topics. However, in this chapter we want to delve into it. We evaluated these kinds of questions in our own lives and in our parenting decisions. In doing so, we realized that there were many, many activities our children could be doing that were beneficial and positive. They would draw our children's hearts to the Lord and to their family. "And whatsoever ye do in word or deed, *do* all in the name of the Lord Jesus, giving thanks to God and the Father by him" (Colossians 3:17).

A key ingredient in what we would do with our time involved being with our children. We knew that we could not protect them from wrong influences or even evil itself if they weren't with us. Therefore, we made it our goal to involve our children in our lives, work, and ministry. Perhaps if we share specifics from our experience it will help you as you pray about and evaluate your own possibilities.

Children's Church Program versus Widow Ministry

When our oldest children were elementary age, we found a Bible-believing, like-minded church that we loved. This church had a Wednesday night children's program in which we quickly involved our children.

It wasn't long until we became aware of some problems for our children and family. The children looked forward to their Wednesday night program for the game time, not the Scripture memory and teaching time. Teri would encourage the children through the week to memorize their verses to be prepared for Wednesday night. Rather than being eager to work on their verses, the children were resistant.

The children began coming home with attitudes that weren't good toward their siblings and parents. We were seeing a greater level of selfishness and an intense focus on the importance of getting to church on Wednesday night in order not to miss game time. In addition, the children were picking up words and other influences from which we had been sheltering them.

As we discussed and prayed about our concerns, it became obvious that a solution was to stop attending the Wednesday night program. Because the children loved that time so much, though, we didn't want to abruptly pull from them this enjoyable activity.

Prayerfully, the decision was made to substitute a widow's ministry, as a family, on Wednesday nights. There was a widow in our church, Ola Mae Clifton, whom we had come to love. We asked her if we could visit her on Wednesday evenings and also help out around the house. Mrs. Clifton was eager to have company and quickly agreed. After gently and lovingly discussing with the children our concerns about the Wednesday night program and telling them what we would do instead, we began going to Mrs. Clifton's house on Wednesdays.

The conversation part was easy. That is what Mrs. Clifton wanted us to do — sit and talk. We had to work harder, though, to get her to give us house projects. Often, we observed a need ourselves and then talked her into letting us fix it. For example, one evening we noticed a light bulb above the bathroom sink was burnt out. Steve offered to change it and any others.

Another time, we could see that the yard needed to be raked. We set up a lawn chair for Mrs. Clifton in her garage so she could watch the work in progress. Teri sat beside her to keep her company while Steve and the children raked the yard. Even after we had moved from Mrs. Clifton's state, the Lord gave her a trip to visit relatives in our new area. We again had the opportunity to have her as a guest in our home, as she had been several times previously.

Consider with us how this change of our time usage helped us keep our children's hearts. No longer were they being drawn to the fun and games of the church activities. Instead, they were being pulled toward one of the goals we had for them – learning to love serving. While the children missed game time at church, they soon came to enjoy helping Mrs. Clifton. They again looked forward to Wednesday nights, but now it was for a better reason. We saw this as the beginning of them having purpose in life.

Nursing Home Ministry

A church we were attending began a twice-a-month nursing home ministry. There were many who participated and supported this ministry in the beginning, including our family. The service was the first and third Saturday afternoons at 1:30 p.m. Steve would take all the non-napping children with him. After several years, the Maxwells were the only ones who were still carrying on the ministry, so it became our ministry. That no one else stayed with the nursing home ministry was disappointing to us, but the Lord had been training our family for serving and ministry together. This was certainly an ongoing opportunity for that.

Here are two verses that strengthened us in the nursing home ministry. "Blessed *is* he that considereth the poor: the LORD will deliver him in time of trouble" (Psalms 41:1). "Pure religion and undefiled before God and the Father is this, To visit the fatherless and widows in their affliction, *and* to keep himself unspotted from the world" (James 1:27).

Steve said when he entered the nursing home, he would send his arrows (children) down one hall and then the other. They would visit the rooms and ask the residents if they would like to go to church. As those who answered positively were wheeled into the dayroom, they would be greeted by the lively notes of gospel music played on the piano by Christopher. Steve would preach a simple message, and they would sing hymns. After the service, Steve and the children talked with the residents.

Carving a chunk of time out of two Saturdays per month was not easy for our busy household. However, it wasn't all giving on our part. The Lord bountifully gave back to us in blessing all that we invested. This was a part of teaching our children that serving is a rewarding use of their time. It allowed them to learn to be comfortable around elderly people. The children have prayed for many years, specifically by name, for their old friends in the nursing home. The boys had opportunity to begin learning to preach. All of the children could use their musical gifts. The nursing home ministry was a continuation of the children having purpose in life – a purpose that was God-honoring.

City Union Mission

We have mentioned previously Steve and the boys' involvement one Saturday a month at City Union Mission. This ministry began for our family after City Union Mission presented its work at our church during a Sunday night service. Nathan, our oldest son, who at that time was about 19 years old, began to feel God directing him to volunteer at City Union Mission.

Nathan was working in downtown Kansas City and could easily stop by the mission one evening a week. He began by offering to help those who ran the mission with their computers. It wasn't long before he was involved in discipling one of the men who had entered the mission's year-long discipleship program. Occasionally, Nathan would be asked to preach at the nightly service if the scheduled speaker didn't show up.

Eventually, Nathan was led to take responsibility for one of the Chapel services that are given out to local churches. The monthly participation in the mission service includes preaching, leading songs, singing, talking to the men, and whatever lunch tasks are needed to help serve the mission men their food. The girls participate in this ministry as well by providing homemade chocolate-chip cookies. They used to experiment with different kinds of cookies, but the men's favorite was always chocolate-chip. The cookies are baked at home and wrapped in cellophane with a Scripture verse included with each one. Often the men eat their giant cookie and come back through the line for another.

This ministry helps our children toward our biblical goals for them in several ways. They are actively learning to share Christ, preach the Word, be ambassadors for Christ, and serve others. The mission time enables them to develop a compassion for others who aren't like they are. It also allows them to see firsthand, in real life, the consequences of wrong choices.

Homeschool Support Group

For ten years we led our local homeschool support group. While Steve and Teri invested the most time in this ministry, the children were highly involved as well. This was a perfect activity to build the children's skills while helping them learn the value of serving others.

When we took over the homeschool group, the first thing we needed to do was to begin producing a monthly newsletter for communication with our group. Nathan was assigned the task of editing the newsletter. We purchased a book to help him learn the word processor we were going to use and gave him the text for the newsletter. He went to work learning how to format a newsletter on a word processor. Several years later, when Nathan graduated from our homeschool and began to work full-time, Sarah took over the newsletter editing.

Christopher developed a website for the homeschool group. With the website, we could have basic information available for those seeking to learn about homeschooling or our group. In addition, Christopher was the organizer and impetus for the yearly spelling bee.

The children often accompanied us to meetings. Sometimes an older child stayed home to babysit younger children. For several years, the older children organized a young children's program that ran during the bi-monthly couples' meetings we had. This allowed both parents to attend the meeting.

Finally, the Lord directed our family away from leading the homeschool support group because of other ministries He was directing us toward. Then the children became a part of those new ministries as well. They travel with us when we speak. They help with the set-up and tear-down of our booths. They enjoy meeting and talking with people who stop by to visit our table. They make sure Dad and Mom have all their materials when they speak and collect those materials afterward so Dad and Mom can talk with people.

The Benefits of Family Service

Having our children involved in ministries the Lord has given to our family allows them to have purpose in life – purpose in serving the Lord by serving others. All of these activities are small things individually, yet they bring the positive influences we want for our children's lives. Each one is a stepping stone for helping our children learn to take joy in serving others rather than wanting to be entertained. This gives them purpose in life because they are being useful.

These ministries helped fill our children's time so that they were too busy to want to "hang out with the kids." Rather than being off with other young people, our children were ministering with their family. This allowed us to know what they were doing. We were with each other, forming an accountability that was good for all of us. We could observe their hearts as they served. It drew their hearts toward their family, giving us purpose as a family unit. Serving as a family met the goals we had for our children while not drawing their hearts away to their peers, to entertainment, or to immorality.

As you walk down this path, the Lord will probably not lead you into the exact same ministries that He did our family. Our desire in sharing the specifics of our ministries is to spur your thinking concerning where the Lord might be directing your family to minister. What are the needs? How can you, as a family, meet those needs in service for the Lord?

We would encourage each of you to begin praying about what ministry the Lord would have you be involved with as a family. Consider a nursing home, the homeless shelter, a weekly Child Evangelism Club for neighborhood children, a neighborhood Bible study, an outreach to a widow, or having neighbors in for dinner – that's just a start! When you have the Lord's direction, begin to serve. You will have no concern about isolationism, but rather you will experience outreach within the sheltered environment of family ministry.

Questions

1. Are you currently serving as a family in any way?

2. Do you know any widows who have needs?

   a. Have you considered offering to help?

   b. Could you include your children?

3. Are there any other areas you can see where you could minister as a family?

4. Do your children have any talents you could employ in ministering to others?

◆ ◆ ◆ ◆ ◆ ◆ ◆

Growing up was great for me. I loved to spend time playing, reading books, and generally having fun doing things children do. I played with my siblings during our free hours. Christopher

◆ ◆ ◆ ◆ ◆ ◆ ◆

Chapter 16

Encouraging Toward Other Positive Influences

When you think of a monastery, what do you picture on the faces of those who live there? What about when you visualize photos of people from religious homes of the past? We expect you imagine solemn-looking faces with a hint of sternness in them but no smiles. Certainly there is no expression of joy in these countenances. That is not the home environment we want if we are to keep our children's hearts.

We have talked already about many negative influences we choose not to allow into our children's lives. Some families may then wonder what exactly the children are to do with their time. While ministry may be an obvious beneficial use of time, one can't spend every minute of the day in ministry. For all the negative things we traded away, there were wonderful, uplifting, worthwhile, positive activities to take their place. For us, this has been one of the most exciting aspects of our journey in learning about keeping our children's hearts. As a family we lost nothing while gaining everything.

Our homes must be filled with the joy of Jesus Christ. For example, Nehemiah tells us ". . . the joy of the LORD is your strength" (Nehemiah 8:10). One of the fruits of the Spirit is joy (Galatians 5:22). Joy is to be manifested in our homes. Part of the way that joy will be expressed is through the positive influences of what we allow there. If we will choose to shelter, our home can be a happy, wholesome environment for our children.

Walks, Reading, and Games

Think back to our discussion of turning our hearts toward our children. Part of that process involved investing our time in their lives. This means when we have time together as a family, we will have family activities. One thing our family loves to do is to go for a family walk. On Sunday evenings, since we don't have Sunday night church, we have several hours of family time. Weather permitting, the children will invariably ask to go for a walk. This interest in family walks did not come about because we gave them an appetite for television. No, we have sheltered our children from TV. Rather, their love for family walks grew because the positive appetite for being with their family was developed.

Reading out loud can be a great way to spend time keeping our children's hearts. Teri has made it a habit for many years to read to the children. The children tell her that she is the best reader in all the world and that one of their favorite activities is to listen to her read. Is she really the best reader in the world? Only to our children! However, the consistency of her reading to the children has created a warm, loving atmosphere in our home. Was the children's appetite for listening to Mom read books developed by renting the latest video to watch as a family each weekend? No, we have avoided those negative appetites while building positive ones by how we have directed the children's time.

Consider occasionally getting out a wholesome board game and playing with your children. Here again, we are sheltering our children. We are keeping them from the negative appetite for entertainment that will come if they sit alone playing video games. Instead, we are giving them the positive appetite for family interaction.

Hospitality, Sibling Friendships, and Creativity

Our children love to have others over for dinner. We can invite a family from church with lots of children over or the neighbors without children. It really doesn't matter. The children will be excited because they like having guests. We have sheltered the children from participating in outings and activities of their own by themselves. Instead we have chosen to have fellowship as a family, with singles, couples, or other families. In the process, the children have developed positive appetites for sheltered fellowship through hospitality. "Distributing to the necessity of saints; given to hospitality" (Romans 12:13). This is a great use of our time. Whether we are ministering to unbelievers through hospitality or fellowshipping with those who are like-minded, we invite our guests to join us for our family altar time while they are in our home.

We want to build strong relationships between the children. This can happen by encouraging them to spend time with each other rather than with others. When our older children were younger, before we began sheltering as we now do, we found that the more they played with friends, the less nice they were to their siblings. They seemed to always prefer to be with a friend rather than their own brother or sister. Their attitudes toward each other were more unkind and sarcastic. Through sheltering from the negative influences of friends, we have gained the benefit of solid brother and sister relationships.

Our children are each other's playmates. We have been pleased to see the older children wanting to continue in those relationships. It is a weekly occurrence for one of the older children to take a younger child out to lunch. Also, the older children will almost always take a younger child with them when running errands. Sibling friendships last a lifetime. Other friendships seldom withstand the test of time.

Teri's mom often tells her our children are the most creative children she knows. This isn't because our children are brighter than others. Instead, we think the creativity they exhibit comes because they have grown up in a sheltered environment where they have learned to use their creativity for play. They haven't been entertained during their free time by the television. Instead the children have played hours upon hours together. It is common to see all five of our younger children playing together, having a delightful time.

Work Projects

One of the most positive influences for our children's lives has been learning to work. As we have turned our hearts toward our children, we have seen the value of including them in the work projects that we are doing. This gives us time together while building valuable vocational skills in their lives. It also allows them productive use of their outside-of-school hours.

Children can be involved in working with Dad or Mom from very young ages. Their enthusiasm for helping and accomplishing a task is boundless. While it is generally quicker and easier to do a job by ourselves, at least when the children are young, we miss the blessing of helping our children learn the joy of working if we make this choice.

This past summer, a family in our church was haying. The oldest son, who would normally shoulder the workload with his dad, was away during the week the baler was available. The men and boys in our family volunteered to be farmhands each evening for the week. Moving hay bales from the field to the barn was hot, dirty, backbreaking work. On one of those evenings, our family had a previously planned social activity. The boys wanted to skip the "fun" so they could work at the farm.

In time the children become productive workers in their own right. Just tonight, our thirteen- and fourteen-year-old boys asked permission to replace the handle that opens their window. Steve wasn't sure whether they could do the task alone, and he wasn't available to work with them at that time. The boys assured him that they could follow the directions. Not long after receiving the go-ahead, Joseph and John were back upstairs eagerly exclaiming how well their window crank worked and wanting their dad to examine their project.

"Train them to a habit of always redeeming the time. . . . No created being was ever meant to be idle. Service and work is the appointed portion of every creature of God." (J. C. Ryle)

For more in depth information regarding Steve working with his boys, we encourage you to read Steve's book *Preparing Sons to Provide for a Single Income Family* (see page 274). Steve shares details about various projects he has done with our sons from age three on up.

Outings and Vacations

Another consideration in keeping your child's heart and in sheltering him will be your choice concerning outings and vacations. We have come to realize that even this time is critical and affects appetites. Many years ago, we went to amusement parks. They were fun. However, we were exposed to worldly music, immodesty, and sometimes evil themes. In the process, we gave the children an appetite for exciting, worldly entertainment.

This was an area that changed for us as we began to evaluate whether our activities were consistent with our biblical goals and what appetites were being created in the children. We found there were alternatives to amusement parks. We could go to the zoo if we wanted a day outing. If we went in the fall or spring, immodesty wasn't as much of a problem as it was in the summer. There were no evil themes if we avoided going at Halloween time.

We also plan vacations with our goals in mind. Taking our children for a beach vacation when the weather is hot would not be sheltering them from negative influences. We couldn't expect our boys to be around women dressed in indecent swim attire and not think their appetites would be whetted for things we don't want them dwelling upon. Once, while on a speaking trip, we were gifted with a night and day at a beach house in South Carolina in January. Those hours at the beach were consistent with our goals because it was quiet, relaxing family time. Since it happened in January, the other people on the beach were dressed for cold weather.

Going to the mountains, where we can rent a cabin for our family, is a perfect place for a vacation. In the mountains, it is cool enough that people will have a far greater level of modesty than would be seen at the beach. At the mountains, the pull and glitter of the world is left behind for the glories of God's creation. We are alone as a family without the interruptions of telephones, work, and computers. Rather than our vacation growing an appetite for all the fun and thrills one can get, it develops an appetite for rest, family time, and glorying in God's handiwork.

What Will You Do?

It is our desire that by giving you examples from our lives of how our time is spent, you will begin to see possibilities for positive influences for your children. The scope of activities with beneficial influences goes far beyond our personal experience. You can evaluate your activities based on your goals for your children and the appetites that will be developed. If your activities hinder sheltering your children or are inconsistent with your stated goals, then we would encourage you to find new ones.

We want our home to be a place of joy. Getting rid of the television and video games while encouraging family activities generates an atmosphere of warmth and love. This is a place where we see hearts being kept and positive appetites developed. Sheltering is in place, and joy abounds.

Questions

1. How does your family spend time together?

   a. Are these positive influences or negative ones?

   b. Are there better uses of your family time that would facilitate your goals?

◆　◆　◆　◆　◆　◆　◆

We have chosen to live without television. By obey-
ing the Lord and not watching TV, my parents
removed what most certainly would have been a
stumbling block to my marriage. Both my wife and
I are grateful for that because we agree that if I'd
have grown up with TV, we'd have one right now
and would waste many hours in front of it.
Nathan

◆　◆　◆　◆　◆　◆　◆

Chapter 17

What About Young-Adult Children?

As children grow up in a home focused on keeping their hearts, what happens when they become adults? Do we continue to shelter? Do we want to keep their hearts until marriage? Should they live with their parents? While this may appear to be a topic relating to only a few, in reality, parents with children of any age will someday be facing these situations. We would love to give parents of young children a vision of what it can be like when their children grow up and still live in their home.

Benefits of Living at Home

All three of our older children have chosen to live at home until marriage. The oldest married at age twenty-five. The other two are twenty-four and twenty-two at the time of this writing, and they are both still at home. It is our desire that by sharing our thoughts and experiences with adult children living in our home, you might be challenged and motivated concerning your future with your own adult children.

We have personally seen benefits to having children remain at home until marriage. Scripture says that a man leaves his father and mother to be joined to his wife (Genesis 2:24, Matthew 19:5, Mark 10:7, Ephesians 5:31). This is why we believe it is biblical and beneficial for adult children to live in their family homes, with parental counsel, until marriage or until the Lord calls them to something such as mission work.

There are fewer temptations with the accountability of living at home in a family. Sheltering is still occurring through this accountability. We see this as very positive. For example, many godly men and women who travel go with their spouse, an adult child, or a friend. Why? Because they know the temptations that even spiritually mature adults face. How much greater would such temptations be for younger, less mature men and women?

In living at home, adult children benefit from our counsel. Because we have been walking with the Lord longer than they have, they seek our advice on decisions they are making. There is time for talking and discussions. Giving and receiving counsel will happen naturally in the course of these daily interactions.

On the practical side, our adult children's living expenses are low since we provide them with room and board. This allows them to set aside money for their future family needs. Our boys saved enough to purchase homes debt-free. What an amazing thing to be ready for marriage and able to buy a home without borrowing! It was such a blessing for Nathan. Christopher now has the finances for his house, as well, should God lead him to marry.

In addition, as our adult children remain in our home, family ties and relationships are maintained. We enjoy watching twenty-two-year-old Sarah help eleven-year-old Anna learn to sew or fourteen-year-old Joseph pitch in to wash twenty-four-year-old Christopher's car with him. Problems between an adult child and a younger sibling still arise from time to time, of course. These provide rich learning opportunities to grow in grace and love, all within the shelter of our home.

Practical Aspects of Living with Adult Children

Our adult children have their own personal schedules for their work and free hours. They confirm matters of schedule with us, though. For example, prior to Christopher booking a photography commitment, he will check to see if there is a conflict. We have had to learn to give the same courtesy back to them. As parents making the decisions for the family, we have been used to making appointments, even family ones, but needing only to tell each other. Now we try to make it a point to let our adult children know what we have committed to so that they can plan accordingly.

Our adult children participate in the family's life. They join us for our evening Bible time almost without fail. We will often discuss evening schedules at dinnertime to make family devotions the most convenient for everyone. We eat lunches and dinners all together, again working to accommodate various scheduling needs. The older children have been willing to continue to contribute to the household workload, maintaining chores they had when they were younger. Steve still has weekly one-on-one sharing time with Christopher and Sarah.

Parenting adult children who live in our home is a relatively new experience for us, since our oldest child is 27 at the time of this writing. We are all still learning how our new roles work. For us, as parents, this has meant we have needed to let go of being in authority in our adult children's lives. Instead we are now counselors and friends – roles that were developing and growing throughout their childhood.

Steve admits that when differences have come up relating to our adult children, he has found it difficult to let go of his fatherly authority role and simply use his fatherly influence. We have made mistakes, but we all continue in the bonds of our family love, looking to the Lord for help and direction, with the goal of growing, working, and serving together.

We have found these years to involve daily opportunities for us to interact with each other in mutual respect. We realize our adult children are to be treated as the adults they are. We are desirous that our relationships with them be characterized by love and deference. "Iron sharpeneth iron; so a man sharpeneth the countenance of his friend" (Proverbs 27:17).

When our children are babies, we shelter them in almost every aspect. When our children are adults, they make their own sheltering decisions as they continue to learn how to rely on Jesus Christ. We have observed in their lives that they have adopted most, if not all, of the sheltering standards they grew up with in our family.

We no longer control our adult children's lives, but we do have a position of influence over them when they are living at home. Decisions are often discussed as friend to friend because they come to us and want our input and counsel. Frequently, it is appropriate to evaluate Scripture that relates to a situation. We then talk about it, pray about it, and discuss it some more. Almost always we come to a decision in harmony. We believe this is because we have been able to keep their hearts.

We do not discipline our adult children. The adult child is responsible to the Lord for his decisions. Having our older children's hearts makes it possible to influence their decisions, but we no longer give consequences for bad choices. Consequences at this point, if there are any, come from the Lord.

Keeping Hearts Until Marriage

For us, marriage is the culmination of keeping our children's hearts. If the Lord calls the adult child to marriage, this is the time that we want to transfer his heart from us to the spouse. The whole process of keeping our child's heart has been for the purpose of always directing his heart to

Jesus Christ. For an earthly relationship, we have worked to keep the parent-and-child relationship the strongest one. Upon marriage, that changes to directing the child's heart toward his spouse.

As we observed this process in our son, we realized how appropriate and right it was. Rather than leaving home and facing the world's temptations on his own, Nathan was being joined to his wife. Now as a couple with hearts turned to the Lord, they would meet the world's pull together. The sheltering of one family was traded for the sheltering of another.

Ecclesiastes 4:12 says, "...a threefold cord is not quickly broken." Nathan, his wife, and the Lord were a much better combination for keeping his heart than Nathan would have been out on his own. After Nathan's marriage, we understood much better the verses about marriage such as, "Therefore shall a man leave his father and his mother, and shall cleave unto his wife: and they shall be one flesh" (Genesis 2:24), and how they related to the transfer of a heart.

As They Grow

We are far from being perfect parents, with learning still continuing in our lives. However, as fully as we could, we have given our hearts to loving Jesus and applying His Word in every aspect of our lives, including raising our children. We wanted to keep their hearts and to shelter them. This often led us to make different decisions concerning the children than other parents were making. Despite those who told us it would never work, we have experienced the joy of watching our three oldest children grow through their teen years and into young adults without rebellion or even major problems. The Lord has clearly been working in their lives, and He gets all the glory for where they are today.

We have had such joy in having our adult children live in our home. Certainly, there are times of disagreement, but with the Lord's help, we work through them. Sheltering and living in the family home have provided added accountability and helped our adult children remain pure. We have personally observed the benefit parental counsel has been in these children's lives.

We have loved moving from a role of authority to a role of counselor as our children became adults. We enjoy conversations and time with our adult children. We see them growing in spiritual maturity, and we often seek input from them on our personal and family decisions. We desire that they feel loved, sheltered, valued, and wanted in our home until the Lord calls them to be married. We would be delighted to see your homes blessed, as ours has been, if your children are living at home as young adults. For us, it has all been a part of keeping our children's hearts and sheltering them.

Questions

1. Do you want your adult children to live in your home?

2. How do you see your parenting role changing as your children become adults?

3. Are you working toward that role change?

♦ ♦ ♦ ♦ ♦ ♦ ♦

I believe my relationship as an adult with the Lord, a relationship that is real and alive, has been significantly, positively impacted because my parents aimed at keeping my heart and then directed it to the Lord. Nathan

♦ ♦ ♦ ♦ ♦ ♦ ♦

Chapter 18

From Those Who Have Lived It

Sarah
(age twenty-two)

I was so excited when Dad and Mom asked if I would be willing to share with you from my experiences growing up with parents who wanted to keep my heart. I pray that this will be an encouragement to you as you seek to keep your children's hearts.

Pre-sheltering Regrets

As I look back over my childhood years, I have several regrets. The first vivid one was a bad experience at a sleepover. This was before my parents began to shelter us from sleepovers. My parents were very careful as to whom I was allowed to spend the night with, but unfortunately, even at this friend's house, things happened that I regret. While it was nothing immoral or really awful, I knew it wasn't what my parents would have allowed, and I still have the negative memories.

My second regret would be the majority of my neighborhood friends. Many of my memories of play with neighborhood children are ones I wish I could forget. My parents were in the early stages of realizing they needed to shelter their children. While they screened our playmates to some extent and wouldn't allow us to play in some families' homes, that was as far as the sheltering went in this area. I'm thrilled Dad and Mom have learned the importance of sheltering the children and that my younger brothers and sisters will not have those same kinds of regrets that I have. My younger siblings have never done sleepovers or played alone with neighborhood friends.

Sheltering with No Regrets

My tendency has been to want to please others and let myself be influenced in ways that would not be good for me. Dad was always right with his encouragement to me that just because "all the other girls did it" didn't mean I had to. His and Mom's sheltering saved me from being swayed by others and making choices I would have regretted during my teen years. I can't imagine where I'd be now if my parents had just let me do whatever I wanted. I wouldn't change their sheltering for anything in the world!

I did not get my driver's license until I was nineteen. At that point, Dad requested that I always take a younger sibling with me when I went somewhere. I admit, at first I was reluctant. I soon realized that it wasn't so much the accountability, but it was for my protection as a young, single woman. I have been very grateful for that in several instances. My siblings love to go places with me. Because of keeping my heart and their trust in me, my parents don't fear I'll go places I shouldn't. When I want to go somewhere, I don't have to ask their permission. As a matter of courtesy, I inform them of where I plan to go and when I think I might be home. Only a handful of times have they asked me not to go – and that was because of a previously made commitment they had.

Communication

I think one key to keeping my heart was my parents making sure they had an open line of communication with me at all times. Dad had a weekly meeting with me each Sunday (as mentioned in Chapter 7), and he still does. I feel free to share whatever struggles I am having and know that he will give me direction, encouragement, and sympathy. I don't want to hide anything.

Mom has cultivated a wonderful mother-and-daughter relationship with me. She made it a priority about seven years ago to have a "date" with me each month (as mentioned in Chapter 6). She often comes in to my bedroom as I prepare for bed, and we talk. Frequently throughout the day, she'll stop what she's doing and sweetly listen to me. She knows I love to chat, and she makes it a priority to listen.

For a few years now, we "older ones" have had Sunday-night talks. After the younger children have been put to bed, we gather in the living room and just chat. Mom has a Sunday-night routine of brushing my hair (which I love!)

and using the electric backrubbing machine on Christopher's back. Our talking time lasts for about an hour, although I don't get my hair brushed that long! Right now, it's Dad, Mom, Christopher, and me. Before Nathan was married, we would always love to hear his courtship or engagement news. Sometimes we'll talk seriously, and other times I'll be in stitches with giggling.

Purpose and Direction

Dad and Mom have given me purpose and direction in these young-adult years of my life. I enjoy working in our family ministry and helping at home, and I just finished writing a children's reading book, *A Summer with the Moodys.* Dad and Mom are tender, understanding, and loving any time I am struggling. They have encouraged me to trust the Lord for everything.

I love being able to serve and minister to others. Through the years, the Lord has blessed me with many different ways to do this. From helping a family with lots of younger children an afternoon a week for a year, to making cookies every month for the City Union Mission, to spending about four hours a day moderating several Christian women and girls' message boards, to teaching my younger sister's school, the list goes on and on. Most recently, I took care of five children from the ages of two to eleven overnight while their parents went away to a bed and breakfast. The Lord provides ministry opportunities, and I delight to do it!

Benefits

I don't believe sheltering has hindered me, but instead benefited me. As an adult, I enjoy interacting with others. Sheltering has not rendered me shy, backward, or unable to communicate. I'm completely the opposite! I love to talk with people and share the joy of the Lord. The other day, I was in the orthodontist office with a few of my siblings. Two of the girls who were working on them started talking to me. Among other things, I shared that I worked at home and that I had chosen not to go to college. Then one of the girls shook her head and made a comment to the effect that she would love my life! I felt so humbled and awed. Truly, it's only the Lord and all He has done!

Having a large family has also been wonderful. I love that my parents chose to let the Lord decide how many children they should have. Children are a blessing, and I enjoy being with my siblings. I have fond memories of holding my youngest sister on Sunday afternoons so Mom could take a nap. Not for the least moment do I regret being in a large family, and I pray the Lord may someday bless me with one. Children are a gift from the Lord!

I had the blessed experience of being homeschooled for my entire education. When I was school-age and walked past neighborhood bus stops or drove by the local high school, I felt even more thankful for my parents home-schooling me. I shuddered to think of going to a school. Being homeschooled allowed me to learn at my own pace, spend time with my brothers and sisters, and most importantly, it helped keep my heart.

As I mentioned earlier, my tendency is to let others sway me. Even if I had gone into a school with firm convictions, I'm sure it wouldn't have taken much teasing to have prompted me to let down my guard. I am eternally grateful for my homeschool experience. To be honest, every year when the younger ones start school, I feel a tug in my heart that brings back fond memories of my first day of homeschool each year. It was always fun to get into a new schedule, have new books, and begin to learn new things! I wouldn't consider any other schooling option for my children. I think it was very key to keeping my heart!

Another important area of sheltering has been one of dress. When I was about ten, we made the switch from wearing pants to wearing modest dresses, skirts, and jumpers. Even as an adult, I still show my new clothing to my parents for their input. It is especially important to me that my dad approves of my clothing, because as a man he is sensitive to what could be a stumbling block to other men. I have embraced dressing modestly, and I wholeheartedly love it!

I received Jesus Christ as my personal Savior at the age of five. Through the years, my parents have strongly encouraged and helped me with having an individual time with the Lord each day. I have been blessed to see the importance they have placed on my relationship with Jesus Christ. My love for Him continues to grow deeper through reading His Word, memorizing Scripture, and communing with Him in prayer. I know that my relationship with Him is the most important thing in this whole world! Since Dad and Mom encouraged that love for the Lord, it has kept my heart tender toward Him and what He wants for my life. I think being close to the Lord has been a key part to my parents being able to keep my heart. Thank you, Dad and Mom, for your incredible example and never-dying love for Jesus.

I am also grateful for the godly advice Dad and Mom give to me. Having that open relationship allows me to share with them. Often, I will feel burdened about an area that the Lord has convicted me with or just something that is on my heart, and I need to talk it out with Dad or Mom. They are always willing to listen, offer counsel if I ask for it, and encourage me closer to my Savior.

Please, I beg of you dear parents, keep the hearts of your children. Listen carefully to what my parents are sharing! Truly, truly, truly, it's all worth it. I can't tell you how grateful I am that my parents sheltered my heart! As I shared above, yes, they made mistakes early on as they learned (which haven't been repeated with my younger siblings), but by God's grace they have kept my heart.

Christopher
(age twenty-four)

As you've read the pages of this book, you've learned much about the way I've been raised. I owe a great debt of gratitude to my parents for this upbringing. Anything good in me is a result of Jesus Christ – but He has definitely used my parents to accomplish much of His purpose for me. As I was growing up, I wouldn't have known what "keeping hearts" was. I didn't realize that it was a high priority for my parents. I simply experienced their desire and efforts to keep my heart.

The result of my parent's endeavors to keep my heart has been the development of a strong bond of love and loyalty to them – another way of saying a deep heart attachment. Some of my most challenging decisions have arisen when I was faced with a choice that my parents recommended against but didn't forbid. It would have been easier in those situations if they had simply told me "no." By saying that they didn't feel it was the Lord's best for my life, I was left with the decision. In those situations, my parents' counsel would weigh heavy on my heart and would help me make the right decision.

The decisions in our home were always based on a desire to follow and obey the Lord – not on a list of rules. Halloween, television, sports, and other worldly activities and pleasures weren't eliminated because everyone else at church was discarding them, or because we received a newsletter that talked about doing so. In fact, more often than not, it seemed like our family was the only one making the change. I believe such an example has helped fuel the desire in my heart to obey the Lord, no matter what He may tell me to do or give up.

Another very important aspect that stands out in my mind is the sincerity with which my parents have lived out those decisions in their lives. I can't think of a single time they have requested more of me than they have of themselves. When we quit watching TV, everyone quit – not just the children. Mom and Dad didn't have different standards for their reading material than they did for ours. When we stopped participating in sports, Dad wasn't playing on the church leagues. We work in a home office, and filtered Internet access isn't just on my computer – everyone has it. Dad didn't encourage us to stay out of a youth group and then turn around and spend his time in the local business clubs. One after another, as decisions were made over the years, I watched my parents living out their faith and encouraging me to follow my Lord in obedience.

Television

When I was young, we watched television as a family. During the years we watched TV, programs were carefully monitored to try to eliminate negative and harmful influences. I was seven or eight when it became evident to my parents that there was absolutely no reason to have television programming in our home. Despite careful monitoring, the shows were not beneficial, and the commercials were very unwholesome. I cannot recall anything I saw during my early years of TV watching that has improved or benefited my life.

I could not imagine being raised in a home with television. Knowing myself and my sinful flesh, I am sure that the TV would have exerted a strong, harmful influence on my heart and life. It would have negatively impacted my relationship with the Lord and definitely my relationship with my family. Entertaining television programs would have exerted a stronger draw on my heart than my desire to spend time with my parents or brothers and sisters. Plus, it would have hindered my desire to learn in school and to operate a lawn mowing business. Because of the blessing no TV has been to me, I will not allow television into my future home, should I marry and raise a family.

Sports

I can remember, as a child, having a much stronger interest in team sports than in my relationship with the Lord. Even though I was young when I played baseball, I worked really hard to build my skills – practice, practice, and more practice. If I had diverted a portion of my baseball effort into Scripture memorization, I would have had a valuable treasure. If I had put part of my baseball effort into learning a foreign language, I would have a skill that would significantly ease a possible future transition to the mission field should the Lord call me there.

When I was ten, Dad took me out for a milkshake and explained that he felt it was time to stop playing baseball. He shared his concerns about team sports with me. The primary ones I remember were that he felt we were losing time in the Word as a family and that I was beginning to be negatively influenced by my peers. That was a difficult thing for me to hear, but I could see my dad's sincerity and desire for what was best for me. He asked if I could agree to give up team sports, and I said I could.

Since giving up sports, I have been surprised to discover that I have not missed out on any of the so-called "benefits" of sports. At the same time, I have enjoyed missing out on all the disadvantages. Mowing grass or going for a run has given me plenty of opportunities for fresh air and exercise without the constant risk of injury inherent in most team sports. I learned to participate as a team member by working with my brother in our lawn mowing business and helping Dad with different projects. I experienced true socialization by spending my time interacting with people who are of a variety of ages. In addition, I, along with my parents, was able to selectively choose with whom I would socialize.

When we ended team sports, we also stopped watching professional spectator sports. The sport we enjoyed watching on TV and occasionally in person was baseball. I remember sitting in the seats above the baseball diamond and smelling the aroma of peanuts and beer. We weren't the ones drinking, but the smell was everywhere. I can also remember hearing rock music and people screaming. All of this was about twenty years ago, and I expect each of those areas have become far worse.

At this point in my life, I am very grateful to not be burdened with the addiction to professional spectator sports that affects so many. A winning or losing record, unfair referee calls, or even a trip to the Super Bowl – none of these have any effect on me. I don't waste the two hours a week that so many men spend watching football games during the season. If the football season was to last about twenty weeks and a father watched one game per week, he would lose one entire forty-hour workweek to sports! I know my love for the Lord is stronger today because none of my heart's energy or passion is wasted on team or professional sports, and I'm grateful to my parents for their loving guidance in those areas so many years ago.

Work

My parents also encouraged me to fill my life with positive influences, of which work was one. When I was eleven and my brother was thirteen, we started a lawn mowing business. Not only did this fill a portion of our time from then until high school graduation, but we also made good incomes during the summer months.

We learned how to run a business and work hard. We developed neighborhood reputations for being diligent, dependable workers. We have a file folder filled with letters of recommendation from people whose lawns we serviced. In fact, one letter came from a schoolteacher who works full time with incarcerated juvenile delinquents and whose wife is a public school teacher.

The majority of the skills I use on a day-to-day basis in my current job all began during my teen years. In order to track the finances of the lawn mowing company, I learned several accounting software packages. When we started our family business, I became the financial officer at age sixteen. Photography and website design were the two other skill sets that began during my teen years.

If I had been fed a steady diet of worthless entertainments while I was a teen, I doubt I would have enjoyed working in my business or developing vocational skills. I would have been too busy cramming "candy" into my mouth to bother eating anything healthy. Upon graduation from high school, picking a particular career field would have been a challenge. Then I would have needed years of additional schooling and study. My career would have been greatly delayed and perhaps hamstrung. As it was, I simply put my already-acquired skills to work in our family business and then deepened those skills through actual work experience.

Communication

One of the most important aspects of my parents keeping my heart, I believe, has been a weekly one-on-one meeting. These meetings with Dad started when I was about fifteen and continue at the time of this writing. Our meeting is usually on Sunday and lasts anywhere from twenty minutes to an hour. In the meeting, concerns, issues, problems, or life in general is discussed. Dad often brings up areas of my personal and spiritual life that he thinks I should prayerfully consider. At the same time, he has always been very encouraging for to me share with him any problems or concerns I have about him or any others in the family.

As I think of rebellious teenagers, it seems their biggest complaint toward their parents is often, "They just don't understand!" Dad is always interested in hearing what I have to say about a matter. When I have been wrong, Dad has taken the time to listen and understand me, but then gently explain – from Scripture – why I was wrong. I have found that I couldn't argue with Scripture and a loving parent who had my heart and desired my best.

The Outcome

I know I have been raised far differently from many other homeschooled, Christian young men. I am grateful to my parents for the choices they made to keep my heart and the blessings I have reaped in my life. Looking past all the career, financial, and relationship gains, I know how much my heart has also benefited. Since my parents were "keeping my heart," it wasn't available to pursue worldly distractions: wrong friends, entertainments, TV, immorality, and so many other traps. As a result, I feel I have become more fully prepared and equipped to enter the world to work and minister, as my Lord would use me.

Nathan
(age twenty-seven)

It's a privilege to share a little about my background and upbringing with you. God has done an incredible work in my life, and I am eternally grateful to Him for that. Part of His working has been Him using my parents in shaping and directing me. My goal in these next pages is to discuss some of my experiences in hopes that it is challenging and encouraging to you.

I would like to open with this thought: There are many allurements that present themselves to children, each asking for their hearts. It could be peers, activities, hobbies, or a host of other things. Because my parents kept my heart, I was spared from many of the problems these enticements bring.

Proverbs 13:6 says, "Righteousness keepeth *him that is* upright in the way: but wickedness overthroweth the sinner." That word "keepeth" means to guard, to protect, to observe, and notice this – to be blockaded. I feel like this verse portrays the parent-and-child relationship when the parent has the child's heart. The parent's keeping of the heart helps preserve and direct the child in the way of the Lord. The child may attempt to stray or leave the path, but the strength of the word "keepeth" shows that the straying will be ineffective. Through keeping my heart, my parents were helping me stay in the path of righteousness. Even more importantly, their efforts were setting the foundation of my life and the way I would go. They were training me in following the Lord and serving Him with my whole heart – something I seek to continue.

Sheltering

The concept of sheltering is one that I've grown up with – or maybe more accurately, grown up under. In looking back, it's easy to see how it was a major factor in many of the decisions that were made regarding myself and my activities. However, sheltering wasn't discussed per se. Decisions were prayed about and evaluated, but I didn't hear the world "sheltering" as I grew up.

We were a regular family seeking to follow the Lord and be obedient to His promptings. Dad and Mom analyzed our activities based on their perceived value in accordance with Scripture. We were told when something was harmful. That's no different from what any other parent does who loves his children. Children are not going to be allowed to do something that is considered harmful to them. The difference in my family was that the bar was higher than in many other families.

My childhood is full of happy memories. I don't have regrets about what I could or couldn't do. It feels odd to even write that, but I believe some people would allege that it's not possible for children who are "sheltered" to look back on their childhood with joy. However, I do!

Throughout growing up, I was encouraged in my walk with the Lord. I was challenged to spend a daily time with Him, to be involved in serving others, and to seek ways to grow as a Christian. When parents have the child's heart, they can guide it in right ways and away from that which is harmful. This is what my parents sought to do for me.

Despite the fact that our home was devoid of television watching from the time I was ten, a lot of peer activities, and team sports from age thirteen, I enjoyed my growing-up years. How is it that children raised in third world countries can still have a happy childhood when they don't have TV, team sports, and youth-group lock-ins? The happiness that complements childhood is more a factor of the family following the Lord's will, harmony, and unity than possessions and activities. Possessions and activities are things that the world around us tells us are important. However, our calling is higher than that of the American culture.

The Real World

One thing people are quick to ask of sheltered youth is, "How will children interact with the real world?" I find extreme irony in that question. I don't think sheltering has had an adverse affect on my social skills. In fact, I would have to say that my parents' philosophies in child raising have enhanced my socialization skills. Positive social habits were complimented and encouraged.

Many people think sheltering a child inhibits their ability to function as adults. Just recently, I was working with someone who said, "There's a lot of evil people out there. How are you going to learn how to deal with them?" My answer was that it's a non-issue. You don't need practice to learn how to deal with evil. Where does Scripture teach that? My grandfather has a little saying that goes like this, "You don't have to practice to be miserable." What struck me as funny in my conversation, though, is that this individual, who had also questioned homeschoolers' ability to socialize, was someone who had what many would consider some very poor social qualities. I was standing there thinking, which of us needs socialization help?

Understanding and Acceptance

Picture a sheepfold. I wonder if the sheep are always happy to stay in the fold when directed there? A shepherd, though, makes decisions for his sheep based not on the sheep's wants but on what is best for them. Our heavenly Father does the same for His children. Our earthly fathers seek to follow that pattern as well. Today, as a Christian, I sometimes don't understand the Lord's direction. As a child, there were times I didn't understand how Dad's decisions were for my best.

My acceptance of my parents' decisions can be attributed to them having my heart. Without this, being told "no" when something seemed important to me would have alienated me and caused rebellion. I'm not saying my responses were always what they should have been. However, had my parents not invested in keeping my heart, I can see that I would have rebelled.

One thing that I distinctly remember regarding any decision I didn't like is that I knew Dad had a genuine walk with the Lord. If his decision was wrong before the Lord, the Lord could and would change his mind. While I cannot recall specific examples, there were times when the Lord changed Dad's heart.

While I've mentioned decisions that were hard for me, I don't remember many of those. Some parents are afraid that if they tell their children "no," they will grow up with bad childhood memories. That certainly wasn't the case with me. Why don't I have negative memories? I believe I was able to receive decisions that were weighty and possibly disappointing because my parents had my heart. They presented those choices gently and with an explanation.

The Outcome of Keeping a Heart

Let me spend a brief amount of time on where I am now. First and foremost, I'm happily married and seeking to follow the Lord with my family. Melanie and I together want God's will for our lives and are dedicated to that. I'm employed by Communication Concepts, a small company owned by my Dad, brother and me. My part of the business focuses on small-business information technology consulting.

Working on my own has taught me many important lessons. I don't have the benefit of a team of co-workers that I can call when I get into a technical jam. I don't have a manager to watch over my day-to-day scheduling and appointment booking. I don't have bi-yearly reviews where I'm told how to improve. In many ways, I work for myself. My years of homeschooling prepared me for this. They weren't a hindrance in my vocation; they were an asset.

When Melanie and I were married, we committed to following our own convictions. We knew we were accountable before the Lord for our actions, and that they needed to be founded on Scripture, in concert with the Holy Spirit's promptings in our lives. For example, we have chosen to live without television. By obeying the Lord and not watching TV, my parents removed what most certainly would have been a stumbling block to my marriage. Both my wife and I are grateful for that because we agree that if I'd have grown up with TV, we'd have one right now and would waste many hours in front of it. This is just one example of how a difficult decision Dad and Mom made is continuing to bless me even after I've left their home. It is now my conviction, but it's a conviction for which they laid the groundwork.

One of the things that we did as a family during my growing-up years was spend time in the Word, both individually and together. Dad stressed to us the necessity of a personal quiet time. We children also learned the importance of a family devotion time by Dad's consistency in leading this. That laid the foundation for Melanie and me. We also seek to be faithful in being in Scripture both as a couple and individually.

A Challenge

I'd like to conclude with some encouragement and challenge. How committed are you to raising godly children? Maybe you are like the archer who drew his bow at random and hit King Ahab between the joints of his armor (1 Kings 22:34). Or maybe you desire to have well-directed, well-aimed arrows. The difference between the two is the amount of effort put into the preparation, handling, aiming, and releasing of the arrow. Firing an arrow in a deliberate way is much harder than just letting it go. I used to have a bow and arrow with which I played. It was easy to aim at the sky and release. However, even as a twelve-year-old, I knew that was both dangerous and foolish. Holding still and trying to target something in the distance was significantly more challenging. I believe my relationship as an adult with the Lord, a relationship that is real and alive, has been significantly, positively impacted because my parents aimed at keeping my heart and then directed it to the Lord.

Are you willing to separate yourself and your family from the world? Scripture says that he who is a friend of the world is an enemy of God (James 4:4). It doesn't say which decisions or what sort of lifestyle makes one a friend of the world. Wouldn't it be better to err on the side of consecration and obedience, living a life fully committed to God and His ways? Our family's separation from the world has enhanced my desire to fully serve the Lord in every aspect of my life.

The other big question is, are you willing to invest what is necessary in having your children's hearts? This investment is made up mostly of time, but it could also involve loving them enough to say no at times, to stand up to those putting pressure on your family to conform to what's going on around you.

Raising children to walk "worthy of the Lord unto all pleasing" (Colossians 1:10) isn't easy. It takes a concentrated effort to have their hearts and direct them to the Lord. Children are too precious to lose to the world.

♦ ♦ ♦ ♦ ♦ ♦ ♦

We learned how to run a business and work hard.
We developed neighborhood reputations for being
diligent, dependable workers. Christopher

♦ ♦ ♦ ♦ ♦ ♦ ♦

Chapter 19

Naysayers

As we raise our children with a bent toward keeping their hearts, many will question what we are doing. They will have reasons why they don't believe our decisions are wise. These well-meaning friends and family members may try to sway us from our position and choices. It is a good idea to be forearmed with their concerns and to have an understanding of where their arguments are flawed.

Exposing Them to the World

Many Christians will say to us that if our children are to know how to get along in the world, they must be exposed to it as they are growing up. They believe if a child lives in a sheltered environment, he won't know how to act in a real adult world. The issue of how children are exposed to the world is critically important. This topic is where the rubber meets the road in parenting – we either win or we lose after years of raising the child. We can do what appears to be a wonderful job in raising our children, and when we are close to the finish line, all can be lost.

Our children will be exposed to the world through daily life and family ministry. They will interact with people from all walks of life, but in the sheltered environment of being with their parents. Discussions and Bible time give us great opportunities to help our children see the problems inherent with following the world versus living by the Spirit.

We discovered that, although our children came from a sheltered home, they were still well prepared to interact in the real-world work force. As adults they excelled in their personal and work lives. They had developed hearts of love and ministry for those who don't know Christ as Savior. At the same time, they were aware of the follies of a sinful life style. They were able to have daily interactions with worldly people through the work environment, while not choosing to walk in their ways. In essence, the argument that a child who grows up in a sheltered environment won't know how to act in the real world was proven to be inaccurate by our adult children's lives.

Two Voices

At times we may hear two voices directing us away from sheltering our children. The first voice tells us that the negative influences around our young children are no big deal, and we shouldn't be concerned. It says we can allow children to watch violent and evil cartoons on television, read children's story books that have monsters, witchcraft, and other wickedness, play with toys that are evil and promote killing, and play violent, evil video games without suffering ill effects. This voice will indicate that if our teaching of God's ways is proper, then these other "harmless" influence steal our children's hearts.

Another voice concedes that some of these things aren't good for our children but that there must be balance. This is the way the real world is, and the children need to begin to be exposed to it. They indicate that we should be careful that not too much bad is getting through to our children. Then if we are careful in our teaching of God's Word, the children will come through without any repercussions.

Unfortunately, as we have observed families listening to each voice, neither one appears to speak biblical truth. Rather than producing children who discern right from wrong and choose to do right (Isaiah 7:15-16), we see them following paths of rebellion. Instead of making children who are harmless, blameless, and innocent (Matthew 10:16, Romans 16:19, Philippians 2:15), these children are pulled to the world. The influences that have been allowed into the child's life have not strengthened him in godliness but have given him a view of the pleasures of sin — a view that has enticed him to follow that path and, furthermore, develop an appetite for more.

Can't Know How the Children Will Come Out

Remember this comment from the first chapter? *"We live a pretty controlled life. My wife homeschools, and we keep our children with us constantly. The brethren in my church have children who don't follow the Lord. One of them had all his children slip away. Another had a grandson who was home-schooled, but went away when he got into the work world." A dad of young children*

It can be discouraging to parents who have hearts for their Lord and for their children to think of losing them to the world. Some will tell us that our children will rebel, probably in their teens, no matter how we try to raise them for the Lord. We heard these negative kinds of comments when our children were young. We saw, in the lives of those we fellowshipped with, outcomes and experiences similar to the ones this dad sees in the families in his church.

Our hearts yearned for more for our children. A hunger was planted in us. It was a hunger for godly children who would grow into godly adults without a trail of rebellion and immorality. We decided to put our trust in God's Word – that He Who is faithful and began a good work in our children will complete it (Philippians 1:6). At the same time, we committed ourselves to truly applying God's Word to every aspect of our daily lives, focusing on our responsibility.

For example, look at 1 Timothy 3:4-5, where one of the qualifications for a bishop (elder) is listed. "One that ruleth well his own house, having his children in subjection with all gravity; (For if a man know not how to rule his own house, how shall he take care of the church of God?)" Next, look at Titus 1:6, where the bishop's (elder's) children again determine his qualification for office. "If any be blameless, the husband of one wife, having faithful children not accused of riot or unruly." God said if a man is to be an elder then his children can't be rebellious. In addition, in Titus 1:6 we read that the children must be faithful. These Scriptures teach that if an elder can't raise his children to love the Lord, he won't be able to lead a church, either.

Examine the Witnesses

Let's evaluate carefully those from whom we hear the negative statements that indicate children are pretty much destined to rebel no matter what parents do while raising them in the Lord. In court, under cross-examination, a testimony may be discredited, or thrown out, if there is doubt as to the accuracy of what is being reported by the witness.

The purpose in this case is not to condemn those who have "lost children," because the audience this book is written for are those who still have and want to keep their children's hearts. We can, however, look at the testimonies from these other homes in order to understand and learn from them. Our experience has been that, upon careful scrutiny, there seems to be justifiable reason why, in some families, a child might rebel in his teens and not serve the Lord as an adult.

Just because the men making those statements appear to be godly doesn't mean they actually raised their children in a godly home. Their godly appearance doesn't necessarily mean the men were godly when they were raising their children. It doesn't mean that the men's hearts were turned toward their children. Even if the children were raised by godly men in a godly home, it doesn't mean the children weren't exposed to harmful influences that drew their hearts away.

This has been a subject of great interest to us through the years. As such, when we have met someone with wayward children, we will gently ask the parents some subtle questions while we talk. Our questions will vary, depending on how well we know the family, but the following are representative of what we try to discover.

How was the Lord Jesus lived out in the home? Did they have a daily family worship time? Was it a time the children enjoyed? Did Dad lead it? Did he like leading it? Did they eat together as a family? Did they go to church together? Did Dad, Mom, and the children have personal devotions each day? Was it a good or a dreaded time?

What influences were there to pull hearts away? Did the parents feel like they had their children's hearts and, if not, who did? How much time did Dad spend with the children? Did he have two jobs requiring long hours out of the home? Did they watch TV? Did they go to movies? How important were friends in their children's lives? What did the family do when Dad wasn't working? What did they do for entertainment and recreation? Did they minister as a family? Were the children homeschooled? Were they in a youth group?

Another big issue is to discern if either parent has an angry spirit. Children will not draw close and trust a parent who is angry, even occasionally. We see that this alone can drive children away.

Again, these questions aren't to condemn anyone. Parents who have lost their children's hearts don't need condemnation. They are hurting and want help. These questions we ask can be very indicative, however, of how a child will do through his teen years and as an adult. We hope that the "right" answers don't bring to mind an unattainable, perfect family. If they do, it is perhaps only because the drifting of the current "church" in our country sees what should be normal life for a Christian as extreme. The answers to our questions present a picture of whether Deuteronomy 6:6-7 was being lived out in the home, whether the parent's hearts were lovingly turned toward the children, and what harmful influences were pulling at the children.

Also, we don't want you to think for a moment that we believe that if you follow a simple list of do's and don'ts, your children won't rebel. We aren't saying that at all. James said, ". . . I will shew thee my faith by my works" (James 2:18). The essence of what we try to find out is just how love for the Lord Jesus Christ and His Word is lived out in a home. We believe that is an indication of how real a presence the Lord Jesus had in the home and whether the children will want to live for Him themselves.

As we evaluate the witnesses who say, "You can raise your children for the Lord and still lose them to the world," we may find that there are inconsistencies in these families. It is our desire not to be critical of their personal choices, but rather to observe and learn from them. If we want to keep our children's hearts, these are important issues with which to come to terms. Following Deuteronomy 6:6-7 puts Jesus Christ in the center of all that happens in our homes – the vital key and starting point to keeping our children's hearts.

You Can't Shelter Them Forever

Consider those naysayers who would tell us that we shouldn't shelter our children now because we won't be able to do it forever. This appears to be a very weak argument. There are many things we do for our children that we won't continue to do when they are adults.

For example, we provide our children with food and clothing when they are young. Most parents don't plan to continue that after their children marry. However, this doesn't prevent them from choosing to feed and clothe their children when they are little. As a matter of fact, this is a part of their parenting job. We believe sheltering is, as well.

The foundation we lay for our children through sheltering them means we won't have to shelter them forever. As they grow and spiritually mature, they will put their own sheltering safeguards in place as adults. We have observed how perfect it is when a young adult leaves home to be joined to a spouse. They go from one sheltered environment to another one, enjoying the added accountability of a mate.

Truly, we can't shelter them forever, nor do we want to shelter them forever! The purpose of sheltering is to protect their hearts. As they walk through their teen years without rebellion and moral failure, they are able to use those years in ministry and service. They are not frittering that time away in worldly pursuits.

They Will Embrace the World

A common statement from a naysayer might be: "If you shelter your children, as soon as you aren't looking, they will do everything you have kept from them. I knew a kid who was a preacher's boy. His parents were very strict with him. He couldn't do what the rest of us were doing. As soon as he left home for college, he did everything his parents wouldn't let him do."

We expect almost everyone has heard of a family with a young person like that. Did the parent's sheltering cause the son to embrace what they were sheltering him from as soon as he had the opportunity? We don't think so. It is likely there was much more to it than can be seen from the statements given. Remember our discussion about an elder's children, and the questions we can ask about the family life. Those would apply in this situation as well. If an investigation were made into what really went on in this home, we would most likely find the cause for the son's rebellion.

Train Them Right

The last naysaying statement we want to consider might sound like this: "If you have raised your children properly, you shouldn't have to shelter them when they are teens. They know right from wrong and can be trusted to make the right choices. Your job is more or less completed by the time they are teens. If you can't trust them now, you won't ever be able to trust them."

We have known many families who believed and lived those words. Their children had been raised to know right from wrong but when faced with the negative influences of other teens, these young people gave into those temptations. As we discussed in an earlier chapter, if pastors, elders, and godly adults fail morally, why should we be surprised if our teens do? If we as parents feel such tremendous "peer pressure" from other adults trying to persuade us not to shelter, then how can we think that our children will not give in to peer pressure and temptations?

Do you know what is common in Christian rehabilitation programs—whether it is for someone who struggles with drugs, alcohol, or pornography? Sheltering and accountability will be a major thrust. The goal for those going through the program is to learn how to resist temptations they are facing. Part of that is to be sheltered from those temptations. The other part is to have a high level of accountability. This is exactly what we are offering our children, by sheltering them, to help them avoid these problems in the first place.

Will the Naysayers Convince Us?

Let's read Deuteronomy 6:4-7 one more time. "Hear, O Israel: The LORD our God *is* one LORD: And thou shalt love the LORD thy God with all thine heart, and with all thy soul, and with all thy might. And these words, which I command thee this day, shall be in thine heart: And thou shalt teach them diligently unto thy children, and shalt talk of them when thou sittest in thine house, and when thou walkest by the way, and when thou liest down, and when thou risest up."

This is the heartbeat of the Christian parent. We will strive in our parenting to raise children who love the Lord their God with all their heart, soul, and might. As we teach these words to our children throughout the day, we are not willing to risk losing their hearts. Each statement the naysayers make, as well as the direction they would have us take, exposes our children to influences that may cause them to love the world more than they love the Lord their God.

In many ways this is the choice we see the naysayers setting before us: "And if it seem evil unto you to serve the LORD, choose you this day whom ye will serve; whether the gods which your fathers served that *were* on the other side of the flood, or the gods of the Amorites, in whose land ye dwell: but as for me and my house, we will serve the LORD" (Joshua 24:15). Each of us must make our decision. As for our family, we will serve the Lord!

Questions

1. Can you come up with more fallacies in the naysayers arguments?

2. Have you heard other arguments against sheltering children?

   a. What fallacies are there in these arguments?

   b. What Scripture would you use to refute these arguments?

3. How will you answer naysayers in your circle of family and friends concerning specific areas of sheltering you may choose for your family?

◆　◆　◆　◆　◆　◆　◆

I owe a great debt of gratitude to my parents for this upbringing. Christopher

◆　◆　◆　◆　◆　◆　◆

Chapter 20

Keeping Children's Hearts

We want to keep our children's hearts. Proverbs 23:26 says, "My son, give me thine heart, and let thine eyes observe my ways." While this may sound like an easy, natural progression of a parent-and-child relationship, we have noted this isn't usually the case. Keeping a child's heart requires purpose, direction, time, and effort.

"My 8-year-old son has been difficult since day one. We have homeschooled all along. He obeys on the outside, but has been known to be deceitful and sneaky. He acts like a teenager at times. He will sulk and be moody and discontent. I told my husband today that I didn't think we had his heart. When under fire, he sulks, turns away from us, walks ahead of us, and has a sullen expression." Discouraged mom

"We are a homeschooling family with an 18-year-old daughter. She is in serious moral failure and seems desperate. She is in total rebellion. Substance abuse is involved as well. We fear for her future." Heartbroken parents

"We have been homeschooling our children for 7 years. Recently we found out that our 15-year-old son has not been honest with us. He has been having a secret relationship with a girl at church. We thought he was committed to courtship. We feel like we have lost his heart." Grieving parents

Sometimes we are prone to think that because we are Christians, go to a conservative church, and homeschool our children, we have our children's hearts and they will not struggle with rebellion or peer pressure. We mistakenly believe they won't choose to become involved in activities we don't want them doing. However, this is not always the case.

The Green Grass

Some dads don't think they can keep their children's hearts unless they find a way to work from home. We challenge these dads to begin, right now, doing all they can do to keep their children's hearts with the time they do have at home.

This will mean Dad turns his heart toward his children. Dad is encouraged to spend his time at home interacting with his family rather than on personal pursuits as long as the children are awake. He can work with the children, serve with them, play with them, talk with them, and be their discipler. He will be having personal Bible times and family Bible every day.

There are moms who long for outside-the-home ministries. These moms will build their credentials for future ministry by serving now in their homes. As they fulfill the responsibilities the Lord has given them in Titus 2:4-5 –

which is actually their most important role – they are preparing themselves for later ministry.

Unless moms first turn their hearts toward their children, they will likely fail at keeping their children's hearts. A mom can be home with her children all day, be a home-schooling mom, and still not have her heart turned toward her children. One evidence of where her heart is might be found by asking what she does with her discretionary time and with whom she does it.

If she chooses to spend many of those precious minutes with her children, we see one picture of her heart. However, if she decides to use all of that time on her personal enjoyments, we are left with another perspective of her heart. We are not saying that every moment of her day must be spent with her children and that she can do nothing she might personally enjoy. Instead, we are suggesting that her time usage will be indicative of her heart direction.

What Will It Take?

Sometimes a child's heart will be observed drifting away from his parents. We must then be determined to take action to pull the heart back. This means an evaluation of our relationship. Has anger begun creeping into our interactions with the child? Are we smiling at him? Have we let some negative influences into his life? Is family Bible time being skipped?

One could go back through every part of this book while considering what is responsible for the child's heart drifting.

Winning the heart back may be as simple as lunch with Dad. It may be as difficult as taking a child out of an activity he has been involved in for several years and dearly loves.

It is possible that some reading this book feel they have already lost the hearts of their children. We want to encourage you that there is hope. The Lord is very merciful to help in difficult situations. He can make ". . . beauty for ashes, the oil of joy for mourning, the garment of praise for the spirit of heaviness; that they might be called trees of righteousness, the planting of the LORD, that he might be glorified" (Isaiah 61:3). Perhaps what you have read in this book has spurred you to consider some of the reasons why you don't have your children's hearts. If that is the case, then you can begin now to reverse that process. We would suggest the prayerful implementation of all that we have been discussing in this book, beginning with making sure your heart is fully turned to your children. Any changes you might make will have to be very lovingly and gently presented to the children. In addition, we recommend Dr. S. M. Davis' tape, "Changing the Heart of a Rebel" (see page 284).

Changing Direction

Remember when we mentioned Nathan and Christopher's Little League baseball playing? Baseball season was a looked-forward-to time of year for our whole family. The boys loved playing ball. We loved watching them play. However, the ball seasons were taking their toll on our family. We seldom had family altar during the baseball months because of evening practices and games. While our goals for the boys were for them to be godly, the ball-playing was creating pride in their lives over their accomplishments. They heard words and saw actions that had never been part of their home lives. The boys' hearts were pulled to their coaches and fellow ball players.

The Lord brought an awareness to us that baseball was not in keeping with our goals for our sons. We were developing appetites in their lives that we didn't want for them. It was time to change direction. Changing direction always seemed more difficult to us than going in the right way from the start. Changing direction is better than continuing on a wrong path, but the best choice is to evaluate activities before they are started.

Taking Nathan and Christopher out of baseball was one of the most difficult things we have ever done. Steve took each one individually out for a milkshake. With tears running down his face, he explained what was on his heart concerning our thoughts about ending baseball. Both boys were disappointed, but they understood the reasons and agreed.

While this story seems sad, it has a great ending. We have asked our sons, now that they are adults, if they regret that baseball change of direction that we made. Both say, without hesitation, that they have no regrets. They believe it was a good decision and are glad for it. This would not have happened, however, had Steve taken away baseball and not replaced it with himself.

Goals and Appetites

We have seen that both goals and appetites play a crucial role in keeping hearts. Have you taken time to prayerfully determine the goals the Lord has given you for your children? These goals help you in your daily parenting decisions. Biblical goals will also be instrumental if you desire to keep your child's heart because they will help turn the child's heart to his father and to his Lord.

Each influence our children come in contact with should be evaluated, not only against our goals, but also for any appetites it will develop. Some appetites will pull a child's heart to the Lord and to his parents. However, many appetites do the exact opposite. Appetites are powerful and should not be underestimated. What seems like nothing more than a child's toy may be the beginning of a negative appetite that will plague the child throughout his life. Is it worth it?

The Fruit

Do you remember "Discouraged Mom's" note at the beginning of this chapter? After her sharing her son's struggles with us, Steve talked with both parents on the phone one evening. This family implemented what was shared with them – what you have been reading in this book. Here is what they later wrote to us:

"I have just the most amazing praise! We put our 'prayer caps' on, pulled the children from ALL activities. There has been the most amazing difference in our house! Our eight-year-old

son has become a true joy. He is truly Spirit led at this time. When he does make a mistake, he is crushed, repentant, and desires only that our fellowship be restored. I see NO rebellion, and believe me, I look for it! The peer influences were even a GREATER problem than we thought, and we could only see that from complete separation.

"I just wanted to thank you for taking the time to talk with us. I LOVE having my boys in worship with us! We had some 'training opportunities' at first, but now they are peaceful, content, and obedient. I never want to go back to the old way, and best of all, my husband sees the fruit of this decision, too."
A now joyful mom

Shipwrecked or Serving?

We aren't trying to say that keeping our children's hearts means family life is absolutely perfect. We consider ourselves to be a very normal family. We have happy, active, energetic children. Our children have bad attitudes sometimes. They can be unkind to each other. We don't always respond to them in gentleness or give them the attention they should have. We can become irritated with them or even get angry. However, we see how each of us wants to recognize our sin and deal with it. We believe the negative behavior in our home is greatly minimized, and some is eliminated, as a result of keeping our children's hearts and greatly sheltering them, despite our failures as parents and our children's personal sin.

"A true Christian must be no slave to fashion, if he would train his child for heaven. He must not be content to do things merely because they are the custom of the world; to teach them and instruct them in certain ways, merely because it is usual; to allow them to read books of a questionable sort, merely because everybody else reads them; to let them form habits of doubtful tendency, merely because they are the habits of the day. He must train with an eye to his children's soul. He must not be ashamed to hear his training called singular and strange. What if it is? The time is short, - the fashion of this world passeth away. He that has trained his children for heaven, rather than for earth, - for God, rather than for man, - he is the parent that will be called wise at last." (J. C. Ryle)

Reading this book may bring up a myriad of questions in your mind – perhaps as many as it answered. The length of the book could double if we tried to cover all applications and every question about keeping hearts. We know that isn't possible or our place. We spoke from our personal experience and knowledge of Scripture. We wanted to give an example of what a real-life family with adult children, who haven't rebelled and are walking with the Lord, did in raising their children in the nurture and admonition of the Lord (Ephesians 6:4). It was our desire to show you how we arrived at the decisions we made. It is important when you have questions that you take them to the Lord. This is why we greatly stressed personal Bible reading and prayer. Also, take time for in-depth Bible study on particular issues. Make sure you know the biblical goals you have for your family and evaluate your questions against the goals. The Lord will direct you in dealing with the specific issues you are facing.

Perhaps not a week goes by that we don't hear the story of a distraught family in the throes of crisis because of a teen or young-adult child. This child has been raised in a conservative, Christian home and usually was homeschooled. Yet, at some point the parents lost the child's heart. What factors contributed to losing his heart? It could have been the church's youth group that did it. Maybe it was the television shows the family watched. Perhaps it was the hypocrisy of angry parents who put on a righteous facade at church rather than dealing in repentance with the sin in their lives.

Whatever the cause, the pain in these families is horrendous. The decisions they face have no good solution. What does the parent do when his child announces he is marrying a person who is an unbeliever? How does a family deal with an older rebellious child who is spewing out his anger and venom on the parents every day while the younger children watch? Maybe it is the son who tells his family he can't wait to get to college so he can do everything they won't allow.

We want to see Christian families avoid these situations. It is our desire that their years as a family be joyful ones with unity of purpose and direction. Serving the Lord together, while growing spiritually, should be the trademark of Christian families. For us, keeping our children's hearts has been the key to avoiding the shipwreck many other parents have experienced in their homes. We would be thrilled if every family would see the benefits of what is presented in this book and make the difficult decisions needed to keep their children's hearts.

While the choices we must make, if we want to keep our children's hearts, may seem hard when we make them, they are nothing compared to the anguish of a child pregnant out of wedlock, one in trouble with the law, or one who simply wants to go the way of the world. Are we willing to make the difficult decisions? God's ways lead to joy and peace. We have found this to be the outcome of raising our children in the nurture and admonition of the Lord (Ephesians 6:4) – choosing to do what we can to keep their hearts – our vital priority.

Additional Resources

We offer materials to encourage homeschooling parents and families. Turn the page to learn about them!

Audio (pages 280-284)
Books (pages 270-279)
Websites (page 285-286)

Keeping Our Children's Hearts

To order more copies of this book, you may call us at (913) 772 0392, or visit our web-sites, www.Titus2.com or www.PreparingSons.com.

Managers of Their Homes
A Practical Guide to Daily Scheduling for
Christian Homeschool Families

by Steven and Teri Maxwell

A homeschool mother's greatest challenge may be "getting it all done." *Managers of Their Homes* offers solutions! Responses by families who have read *Managers of Their Homes* and utilized the Scheduling Kit indicate the almost unbelievable improvements they have realized.

Step-by-step instructions and a unique scheduling kit make the setting up of a daily schedule easily achievable for any homeschooling family. *"People have told me for years that I need a schedule, but every time I tried I couldn't get one to work. I always had problems fitting everything that needed to be done into one day. With your system, I am actually accomplishing more, and I have more time left over! The key to it is the great worksheets. They are invaluable."* Who wouldn't like to accomplish more and have time left over?

Managers of Their Homes: A Practical Guide to Daily Scheduling for Christian Homeschool Families sets a firm biblical foundation for scheduling, in addition to discussing scheduling's numerous benefits. Chapter after chapter is filled with practical suggestions for efficient, workable ways to schedule a homeschooling family's days. Thirty real-life schedules in the Appendix give valuable insight into creating a personalized schedule.

"My schedule has given me back my sanity!! I can't believe the way my life has changed since implementing a schedule." Tracy L.

"I had read almost every organizational book there was, and I still couldn't get to where I wanted to be until I applied this method!" Corrie

"In retrospect, having used the book, I would have paid $100 for it, if I could have known beforehand the tremendous benefits I would gain: peace in my busy home, and the ability my schedule gives me to accomplish the things I feel God wants me to do in my family." Tracy

Perhaps *Managers of Their Homes* will provide solutions for your "getting it all done" challenges!

To order or for more information: www.Titus2.com

Or call: (913) 772-0392

You may also e-mail: managers@Titus2.com

Homeschooling with a Meek and Quiet Spirit

by Teri Maxwell

A desire of a homeschooling mother's heart is to have a meek and quiet spirit instead of the discouragement, fear, and anger she often experiences. She can cope with the myriad of daily difficulties and decisions that a homeschooling lifestyle brings with it, as long as she is having the right responses to them. Let her be fearful, worried, anxious, frustrated, irritated, or angry, and this mom realizes she is undermining all she wants to accomplish by homeschooling.

Because Teri Maxwell has walked the homeschooling path for many years, she knows firsthand the struggle for a meek and quiet spirit. The memories from her early homeschooling years of often being worried and angry rather than having a meek and quiet spirit are unpleasant. Her prayer is that as she shares the work the Lord has done in her heart, through homeschooling, you would be encouraged that He can do the same for you. She also desires that you learn from the lessons He has taught her so that you may begin to have a meek and quiet spirit long before she did.

Will your journey toward a meek and quiet spirit be completed upon finding the perfect spelling curriculum or deciding which chores your child should be doing? Or does the answer lie on a different path? In these pages, Teri offers practical insights into gaining a meek and quiet spirit that any mom can apply to her individual circumstances. She transparently shares the struggles God has brought her through and what He has shown her during these many homeschooling years.

In *Homeschooling with a Meek and Quiet Spirit*, you will discover the heart issues that will gently lead you to a meek and quiet spirit. Come along and join Teri as you seek the Lord to homeschool with a meek and quiet spirit!

"Thank you for your Homeschooling with a Meek and Quiet Spirit *book. It touched my heart with all of my struggles as I homeschool my children. Each time I read a new page, I felt as if I was sitting down with a box of tissues, a cup of tea, and a dear, trusted friend. I shed tears as I realized I wasn't the only one who struggles and as I found the rebuke and balm of Scripture to help me work through so many areas. Until I read your book, I was dreading September and the start of another year. I have a renewed excitement and inward peace that the Lord is with me on this journey if I continually seek His face." Susan*

To order or for more information: www.Titus2.com

Or call: (913) 772-0392

You may also e-mail: managers@Titus2.com

Preparing Sons to Provide
for a Single-Income Family

By Steven Maxwell

In today's world of two-income families, preparing a son to provide for a single-income family seems an overwhelming task. Christian parents will find it helpful to have a purpose and plan as they raise sons who will one day be responsible for supporting a family.

Steve Maxwell presents the groundwork for preparing your son to be a wage-earning adult. He gives practical suggestions and direction to parents for working with their sons from preschool age all the way to adulthood. You will be challenged to evaluate your own life and the example you are setting for your son.

As the father of eight children, three of them now wage-earning adults, Steve has gained valuable experience he openly shares with other parents. Learn these principles from a dad whose homeschooled son purchased a home debt free at age twenty-four and whose second son is financially able to do the same. Steve explains how it is possible for parents, with a willing commitment, to properly prepare their sons to provide for a single-income family.

"You are dealing with topics that no one I know of has dealt with as thoroughly and practically as you have." Dr. S. M. Davis

"Preparing Sons to Provide for a Single-Income Family *was a big blessing to my husband. All you ladies should get a copy for your husband and every church library needs one." Shelly*

"Brothers, I highly recommend the book for those of you who have not read it. I really appreciate all the obvious prayer, effort, and experience that went into making this book. The Lord is using it for His Glory in our family." Les

"My husband just finished Preparing Sons to Provide for a Single-Income Family *and came away so motivated and stimulated! He is planning to buy copies for all of the dads on our team and for his brothers! He has been sharing all of the wonderful things he learned and ideas he had on how those principles need to be applied in our family! I am so encouraged! I am usually the one who does reading in light of training our sons, it was so refreshing for him to have been so stimulated. Thank you so much for being willing to write and put your thoughts, convictions and heart in an excellent book!" A missionary wife*

Preparing Sons is available in paperback or unabridged audiobook.

To order or for more information:
www.PreparingSons.com or www.Titus2.com

Or call: (913) 772-0392

You may also e-mail: managers@Titus2.com

Just Around the Corner
Encouragement and Challenge for Homeschooling Dads and Moms

By Steven and Teri Maxwell

Just Around the Corner is a compilation of Steve and Teri Maxwell's monthly Dad's and Mom's Corners. These articles were originally written to encourage and support their local homeschool group. However, they have been so well received that they are now requested via e-mail every month by thousands of homeschool families.

The Maxwells have also been asked to put the Corners together into this convenient-to-read book format. You will find the Mom's Corners grouped together in the front of the book and the Dad's Corners in the back. The Corners are all indexed so that you can read the ones relating to a specific topic you are interested in, if you so choose.

Because most of these articles deal with family life in general, many Christian non-homeschool families find them useful as well. Topics addressed in *Just Around the Corner* include anger, depression, child training, and husbands loving their wives.

Steve's writing will challenge dads in their role as the spiritual head of the family. Teri's writing addresses many aspects of daily life that often frustrate or discourage a mom.

With three of the Maxwell children now adults, Steve and Teri write from the perspective of having seen the truth of God's Word put into practice. At the same time, they are still in the trenches homeschooling five children. You will have a candid vantage point as you see them fail, succeed, laugh, and cry while they endeavor to serve the Lord Jesus Christ.

Now you can enjoy the support and insights found in this unique, indexed collection containing over five years' worth of Dad's and Mom's Corners.

"The Maxwells are so encouraging and down to earth. I had been feeling down about some negative behavior in my children, things in my marriage, homeschooling, and the list goes on. This book has helped me to regain my focus and carry on to what God has called me to do." Michelle

To order or for more information: www.Titus2.com or www.PreparingSons.com

Or call: (913) 772-0392

You may also e-mail: managers@Titus2.com

A Summer with the Moodys

By Sarah Maxwell

A Summer with the Moodys is a children's reading book that follows a family throughout the summer. You will see them help a widow and her dog, Honey, Max, Mitch, and Mollie start two little businesses. With those businesses come some excitement! Little Maddie adds her spark of joy, too. Woven throughout the book is the Moodys' love for the Lord and their fun time together. This is not an adventure book, but rather a family-centered story with godly role models and Christian values.

"*It's not very often that my kids come to me and ask things like, 'Mom, can we have Family Fun Night where we play games instead of movie night Friday?' or, after reading Scripture, 'Can we each pick out a way to apply that?'*" Julie, mom

"*I purchased Sarah's book* A Summer with the Moodys *as a Christmas gift for our children. The older children, ages 10 and 11, have been reading it aloud to our entire family in the evening, and they laugh and laugh. Thank you so much for a wonderful book. Please write a whole series. I would buy them all!" Kathryn, mom*

"I really liked the animals and the idea of Family Fun Night. I like how they did their Bible verses together. And I loved cooking with Mollie! I also liked how they took care of Mrs. Clifton and Honey." Kayla, 8

"My girls loved this book, we read it in just one week. The next week when I got out a new book for our read aloud time they all protested and begged to read the story of the Moody family all over again! As a mother I enjoyed the 'real life' aspects of the book, like the Momma taking needed naps and the children learning to be responsible for chores, etc." Melissa, mom

To order or for more information: www.Titus2.com, www.PreparingDaughters.com or www.PreparingSons.com

Or call: (913) 772-0392

You may also e-mail: managers@Titus2.com

Audio Resources

Anger – Relationship Poison

By Steve and Teri Maxwell

Homeschooling families have a heart's desire to raise godly children. However, it seems that anger is found in many homeschooling parents, and it can undermine all the hours invested in positive teaching. It can destroy our most precious relationships. Have you noticed how certain levels of anger are accepted and justified? Is a little anger beneficial? Do you have difficulty controlling your anger? Is a harsh tone in your voice anger? Are you discouraged by the anger in your life and in your home? Steve and Teri Maxwell will encourage you on this universally needed topic as they share from God's Word and personal testimonies.

One hour. Available in cassette or CD. To purchase, please visit www.Titus2.com, www.PreparingSons.com, or call (913) 772-0392.

Sports – Friend or Foe?

By Steve Maxwell

Many homeschooling families are heavily involved in sports. What are the parent's goals in having their children participate in organized sports? Are these goals being met? Are the children better or worse by being one of the team?

Steve weaves data into this presentation from a large on-line survey that he conducted regarding Christian families and sports. We feel this is a very important message for homeschooling families!

Approximately fifty minutes. Available in cassette or

CD. To purchase, please visit www.Titus2.com, www.PreparingSons.com, or call (913) 772-0392.

Building a Vision

By Steve and Teri Maxwell

Whether new or experienced homeschoolers, this motivational and practical workshop helps a family attain their heartfelt goals for raising and educating their children. Doubts, discouragement, and burnout can easily shipwreck the family that doesn't know "where they are going." What is it that keeps a family homeschooling through a mom's feelings of being overwhelmed, a child with a rebellious spirit, or a house full of babies and toddlers?

Together, Steve and Teri share in this workshop how they moved from homeschooling for convenience (we'll try it a year and see how it goes) to homeschooling forever. They will give you concrete examples from homeschooling struggles they have experienced and how they made it through. With three adult children whom they homeschooled and five more children who are currently being homeschooled, they have the experience to know how to keep on while still being in the trenches of day to day homeschooling

"Teri and Steve complimented each other. They worked well together as a team and were unified."

"It was very encouraging. After 12 years of homeschooling, I needed it."

"Enjoyed the real-life examples given. They are great motivators to continue homeschooling."

Approximately one hour and forty minutes. Available in two cassettes or two CDs. To purchase, please visit www.Titus2.com or call (913) 772-0392.

Loving Your Husband
By Teri Maxwell

One area Titus 2:4-5 tells the older women to teach the younger women is to love their husbands. In this practical workshop, Teri discusses both the starting point and the keys to loving your husband.

Are you a helpmeet or a wife who tries to control her husband? Teri shares many examples from her own life and how the Lord has used them to both convict her and teach her how to love her husband. Join Teri as she evaluates how a meek and quiet spirit can help us be godly wives, building our houses rather than tearing them down (Proverbs 14:1).

Approximately fifty minutes. Available in cassette or CD. To purchase, please visit www.Titus2.com or call (913) 772-0392.

Manager of His Home
Helping Your Wife Succeed As She Manages Your Home
By Steve Maxwell

Do you desire to know what practical spiritual headship actually means? Does your wife long for you to be the spiritual head of the home? How do you lead and still allow her to manage the home?

This two-hour audio session lays down basic principles for spiritual headship highlighting the special needs of a homeschooling family.

Christian fathers will be built-up and encouraged in their role as spiritual leader of the home. Steve uses Ephesians 5:23-29 as a framework for sharing. One husband was overheard telling another during a session break,

"That was the best hour of my life."

We ask that this message be listened to by men only. We would not want to stir up expectations in a mom's heart that might not be fulfilled and then be a source of discouragement for her.

"I would recommend this message to others because it provided plenty of practical, daily examples of how to lead the family."

"I was very pleased with the specifics of how all of this trickled down to practical living."

Approximately two hours. Available in a two cassette album or two CD album. To purchase, please visit www.Titus2.com or call (913) 772-0392.

Experiencing the Joy of Young Womanhood
By Sarah Maxwell

Young ladies, what are your goals in life? Are you waiting for something to happen? Courtship? An exciting opportunity? Sarah, age twenty-one, shares truth from Scripture, her life, and other testimonies about the importance of God-given goals for your life and resting in Jesus. She addresses issues such as having a daily time with the Lord and building family relationships. Sarah also gives practical applications for joyfully serving the Lord and your family. This workshop is geared for young ladies thirteen and up.

Approximately forty-five minutes. Available in cassette or CD. To purchase, please visit www.Titus2.com or call.

Note: We have a special compilation of many of our workshops available in an album for a reduced price. Stop by our web-site or call for more information!

Freedom from the Spirit of Anger
By Dr. S. M. Davis

We feel this to be the most important message you could hear to help you overcome the spirit of anger. Dr. Davis will grip your heart as he shares about this life-changing issue. Even if you just have a "tone" in your voice, it is still anger. Dr. Davis gives ten key steps to find freedom from the spirit of anger. It has helped us make tremendous positive change in our family as we seek to overcome anger.

Seventy-seven minutes. Available in cassette. To purchase or for more information, please visit www.Titus2.com, www.PreparingSons.com, or call (913) 772-0392.

Changing the Heart of a Rebel
By Dr. S. M. Davis

This message is for parents only. We feel it is a very important topic and ties in with the theme of this book. Even if your child is not rebelling, you will glean great insight from listening to this sermon. You'll discover warning signs for which to watch plus a strong resolve to keep your child from rebelling.

Sixty-four minutes. Available in cassette. To purchase or for more information, please visit www.Titus2.com, www.PreparingSons.com, or call (913) 772-0392.

Note: We have several other sermons available by Dr. Davis on our web-site, www.Titus2.com.

Websites

www.Titus2.com

Titus2.com, a website by Steve and Teri Maxwell, is designed to challenge, encourage, and strengthen homeschooling parents. On the site you will find articles, the Maxwells' books, cassettes and CDs, children's reading books, and other resources. There are also sample chore charts and free master lists!

Every month, Steve and Teri each write an article of encouragement and challenge for homeschool parents. To receive the Dad's and Mom's Corners via e-mail, visit www.Titus2.com to sign up. There are also many Corners archived on the site.

MOTHBoard – An Internet message board designed to support moms who are using *Managers of Their Homes* (MOTH). Registration required and open only to those with a registered MOTH book. For registration information, see the last page of the MOTH book.

STUDYBoard – A message board/forum for the discussion of a specific approved book chosen by Titus2. The purpose of STUDYBoard is to allow moms to participate in a study group with other women without leaving home.

MOMSBoard Cookbook – A recipe, cooking, and baking message board information network.

ClassicThreads – Topics of interest for Christian women.

www.PreparingSons.com

PreparingSons.com's purpose is to encourage fathers and sons in the Lord Jesus Christ. It is a clearinghouse for ideas, where fathers and sons can share with others who are like-hearted. There is a message board located on the site – Programmers Forum. You can also read the latest Dad's Corner or sign up to receive them.

www.PreparingDaughters.com

PreparingDaughters.com is designed to strengthen and prepare young ladies in the Lord. We feel there is such a need to offer young ladies like-minded resources and encouragement, letting them know they are not alone in that for which they stand. There is a list of recommended reading books, resources for young ladies, and more areas that are being developed!

Notes

Notes